Journey to Stardom Productions

Smart, Broke, and Want to be a Star

Nicshelle A. Farrow M.A.Ed
Smart, Broke, and Want to be a Star

Contents

Dedication

To my family, friends, readers, and people who want to become a star.

Foreword

If you have ever wanted to delve into a person's life that is also on a journey to stardom, this is the book to read. Embody God, Family, and Career. Dreams may be delayed yet perseverance is ongoing. Lord Willing this book will reach children, parents, churches, schools, libraries, corporate businesses, various media, and movie screens!

CHAPTER I

Star Quality

"Self-doubt drowns your dreams. Hesitation holds you hostage. Skepticism scares away your success. You wonder, 'What will they think?' I don't have a degree or a diploma…[there] is a list of billionaires and multimillionaires who never graduated from college" [or earned a trophy] (Allen & Hansen, 2002.)

Journey to Stardom

While earning my master's degree in Nevada, I attended acting classes to participate in an international talent showcase to be held in Miami, Florida. I completed my master's degree studies and moved to California. I had a promising apartment but with the moving truck outside the apartment manager told me he decided to rent the place to someone else that had California check stubs. He asked if I wanted to see the apartment anyway. What was I to do get mad, cry, go off, or be nice and oblige the offer? As an entertainer, I know how to save face so I did the walk through and left with tears in my eyes as I walked down the stairs to tell my friend and cousin that I needed to find storage because the apartment was rented to someone else.

Silence had fallen over a beautiful day, noisy moving truck, and nearby traffic. I believe, God was telling me something. I did not know what was going to transpire next. I left Nevada where I had two lucrative jobs, lived in a four-bedroom house on my own with savings, and after a few months at my mother's house to save additional money prior to the devastation of not knowing where I would be living. That unknown place became a motel on Figueroa in South Central Los Angeles, California! My whole life had been turned upside down.

My pride would not allow me to ask any family members or friends for a temporary place to stay. I became friends with people I thought I would not encounter because I was always trying to get ahead. I had a long road ahead of me to learn to be more humble than my perception. Now, I purposefully choose when to be more of a listener than a talkative person and schedule when I will be a talkative person. Even until the day my family reads this entire book will they learn why I call less and speak less about my ideas and dreams than once upon a time in my life. Listening is so powerful and you learn so much more. Furthermore, you become more of a healer than a repeated speaker.

After moving my belongings into storage, I settled into a motel room as home while not knowing it would be approximately two years before I would be able to move into a hotel room and then into an apartment. During that time, I did travel to Miami, Florida with my last check of the summer from my Nevada teaching experience. I gained a scholarship to return for the next years' international acting competition as well as an agent. The agent would later introduce me to, Carlos Santana at an Agency Christmas party.

Low and behold, I learned that I was going to need money I did not have for more headshots, clothes, gas money for auditions, and parking fees once I returned to California. I could have walked outside with a 6 foot pole waving a white flag because everyday I just wanted peace but the streets of LA and the pain of wanting to be a star everyday hurt. I was hungry and had too much pride to ask for help. I began to pray more and cry less. Everyone has a plight. Something else I learned that if talking about your plight is more stressful to you, then write which I learned from my cousin, Cherise Roy who I would later collaborate with on three books in one summer.

I began to do background work because they feed you good most of the time while you wait for camera direction. Unfortunately, I was counterproductive because I ate food with no direction. Then, I began to eat healthier foods but by then I had gained so much weight that I was almost 190 pounds and wanting to be a star. Simultaneously, I worked as a substitute teacher and needed gas money until payday. So at this time in my life I had two jobs that were not permanent, living in a motel paying $220 a week, and trying to show my youngest daughter a good time while I felt it was the worst time in my life. The best acting lessons of my life were during that period of my life because I learned to conjure appropriate feelings to display instead of throwing my hands up, falling down to my knees and crying all day long, everyday. I learned the art of saving face that was in all actuality prancing around my pride.

I could not face telling even my parents how bad my finances were especially after recently gaining a master's degree! However, there was one time an inkle of honest feelings was revealed when I met my father and a cousin-n-law at an apartment complex where they were doing carpentry work. After, I had just recently babysat a cat for my brother and his girlfriend while they went on vacation just to stay at their apartment and not have to pay the weekly motel fee. So, yes, I shoveled cat poop for a week every morning before a long-term substitute teaching position within a year of earning a master's degree. In addition to that, I had been living in my car and bathing at a fitness center that stays open day and night. So, when my father and cousin-n-law asked with love and sincerity about how I was doing, my eyes watered, I looked away, and that was enough for my father to reach out and hold me. Tears overwhelmingly streamed down my face and my cousin-n-law looked away. We see babies and people across the spectrum of ages that look away when strong feelings are felt so when you see natural occurrences happening on the big screen that are tear jerkers it is based on natural occurrences in human beings.

Not only does an earthly father that you call Daddy, like I do mine know when to hold his daughter up, he will inquire and let you live your life. It was not long ago that my father told me what to do as a note from a father that has let his daughter find her way through this world. He told me the next job I get meaning a well paying job in education to not let it go. He has given me per se a twenty-year run to try different jobs, take my time with earning a doctorate degree, marry, divorce, have children when all the while he sat there on the side line and let me live my life accordingly so that I would not feel pressured to become this or that. I am thankful for that ideal and his recent advice. Additionally, he knows I want to be a star and is very supportive.

Even while I talked to my parents, family, and friends less due to feeling insecure about my finances and lack of use of my new master's degree, I did not go to jail or do drugs. I prayed to God to keep me safe and free from harm. The harm I was thinking about was physical. I prayed specifically to be free of physical, mental, and emotional harm. Thank goodness, I lived through sleeping in my car in parking lots and major streets including across the street from the very University I received my

Bachelor's Degree. Mentally, I will remember how I felt and will be able to empathize with people enduring financial, pride, and weight gain challenges. Also, I hope to help people who will read this book to be encouraged to press forward during the surprise strong storms that will come into your lives. Emotionally, I am still very close to tears and overcome by tears when I talk about the valleys in my life while all the while wanting to be a star.

More than the money that comes from being a star it is the influence that I will gain and would like to capitalize upon by becoming a motivational speaker for schools. After completing more than half a doctorate program in education instructional leadership, I have not learned of any motivational speakers for schools that are women and have the desire to be a star from acting that grew up in the trenches of Compton, California.

I am blessed to have grown up in a home, reared by good parents of substantial quality, and participated in sports and music lessons. On the other side of the spectrum, I experienced losing school friends due to a flesh eating disease, sickle-cell anemia, drug overdose, and many drive-by shootings all before becoming a teenage employee. Also, I have been blessed to have the right mind to want to be independent. Conversely, I have been challenged with wanting to be so independent that I have let pride overcome me.

What I learned after earning my master's degree and living in a- motel to- a car, back to a motel, and, then to- a hotel was to become humble if not more humble, patient, more thankful, and full of faith and I am still learning.

When I learned from my mother that children are compared. I always wanted to be better and be the star. My brother is better in math than I am and that has propelled me to become an overachiever in areas of strength. Likewise, I learned it doesn't feel good to be compared to a sibling. Later in life, I learned that both my mother and father were singled out as children and just as well harbored childhood pain. Knowing this information about my parents' childhood and vivid memory of the distinction that was made about my intelligence in comparison to my brother based on state educational assessments inspired me to refuse the notion of favoritism amongst students that I have taught and will teach. I carry my parents' childhood pains they shared with me into every teaching situation and I believe they have helped distinctively cultivate my classroom rapport. Also, the responsibility of organization and paperwork skills learned from my mother has assisted me in schools and now I have a Master's Degree in Education Administration and Supervision.

Likewise, my father has assisted me to be courageous, comical, and use my charisma to be an inspirational teacher and future star because I learned to encourage students from where they are in their learning process to the next learning dimension without the pressure of feeling failure. It may not be a science but my parents have taught many lessons that have helped me to inspire many children and have later learned I have inspired many adults as well, so hopefully this book will continue to inspire the band of age groups.

So many times in my life, I have been told that I have a lot of energy. My energy comes from the attention I desire. Even while growing up as well as many other children, I heard, "she wants so much attention." Thank goodness, I didn't grow up with many siblings. I have one brother. Over the course of time I have been complimented on every aspect of my life. It's documented that I am a recipient of Who's Who Amongst America's Teacher for being a math teacher, which delineated a harbored concept that I was not good in math as a child based on state educational assessments. Just think I have always known that I wanted to be a teacher too even since third grade. By the time I went to junior high school, I conceded that math would not be the subject I would be able to teach however the student that nominated me for the revered teacher award was from a student I taught in an algebra class as a first year junior high school teacher.

That experience planted seeds toward performing as a Stand-Up Comedian because I thought teaching would be overwhelming just as many people share how Stand-Up Comedy can be overwhelming but the thrill of the challenge became invigorating to me. Later, I would become a substitute teacher for math classes as well as a math teacher for an adult education school. Nevertheless, state assessments are being improved. In addition, I would encourage parents to continue to focus on the star within their child(ren) especially when discussing results of state assessments because they communicate a temporary evaluation of data.

Do you think people with star quality are overwhelmingly happy people?

Well think about the many comedians you have heard that share the concept that their comedy comes from dark places or unhappy experiences. How about imagining the times you were happy about going somewhere and a special person in your life cancelled on going with you after you were dressed and waiting? Specifically, what if you were winning an award? The above passage demonstrates that even harbored pain can be turned into something great for a new generation.

I Am A Teacher With Star Quality

I was in many school plays. Later, I directed a play at a church and many class plays as a teacher. A decade later, I created my company, Journey to Stardom Productions for the purpose of giving background actors a voice in writing, filming, producing, directing, and principle parts. I am still on my journey to stardom. It takes a great deal of time, money, and perseverance to develop any company. Fortunately, I believe many successes do not happen overnight but many do, it just depends on the alignment of various factors.

Over the years, I have been told that I have star quality and I have always felt it and dreamed of being a star for acting. At one period of time, I wondered if I could be a great singer too like many talented singers in my family. My father told me that he would get me some books about singers. His purpose was to get me to learn the journeys that well-known singers endured. My parents bought an entire set of Encyclopedia Britannica. That was one of many instrumental examples that inspired me to become a teacher. The power to move people through knowledge is powerful.

Talking Aloud To Yourself

Have you heard yourself say aloud, "Let's talk about this?" I have asked myself that question aloud. From my experience it stems from the need to communicate thoughts but not having anyone in my circle that may relate to my concerns or think they have the time to listen because they are busy with their families and careers. For example, I have stood in front of my refrigerator and said aloud, "Is this all I have in the refrigerator?" At any rate, writing a book provides the outlet to speak to oneself whereas communication about the information is simply delayed.

After a Comedy Show

Who likes to celebrate at home alone? You might think all comedians come home and talk about their show. Well, there are many and there are some that I know that practically go home and talk to themselves just to expel the energy. For example, I performed at the Comedy Store in the Main Room on Sunset Boulevard in Hollywood for the first time. First of all my boyfriend flaked on me at the last minute. Ninety percent of my friends/associates cancelled because it was raining and most of them would have had to travel from South Los Angeles, California. The few people that showed were friends of my youngest daughter's teacher and previous co-workers. I went home after a first great gig filled with deep joy to a quiet apartment and thirst to share how much fun I had. Some may wonder, well isn't it the same when I get a chance to talk about my gig the next time I see someone? No, it isn't the same because the adrenaline is gone, I'm not dressed-up, the person isn't an actor, or have not experienced the many rejections before landing a gig that makes all of the other rejections miniscule. However, I am very thankful to those that have taken the time to inquire and listen.

Smart enough to earn a master's degree but broke financially.

I want to be a star so that my voice is heard by millions and to earn enough money to pay off mortgages, buy reasonable cars, have savings, and no worries about a budget to eat and drink healthily.

Why Wear Wigs and Weaves with Beautiful Hair?

Many stars wear wigs and weaves. I wear wigs and weaves to add volume to the star within that is waiting to shine. I was on ABC with a weave that you really could not see because I had a helmet on in a racecar but I would like to think if I wore my own hair that is thin the helmet would not have stayed on. I ponder, will I cut my hair short and wear it low on the nape of my neck after I have reached stardom like so many other actresses have done. It seems as though the more the age and money you make the less hair you choose to wear or is it stress that comes along with stardom?

Jealousy or Lack of Communication

When people sway to negativity about your accomplishments is it jealousy or lack of communication? Aside of writing this book in the hopes that it will be a voice for people who have shared similar experiences and desire to be a star; I have learned to speak less about my accomplishments and cater more to the person on the other end of the phone or conversation. Based on my experiences, I gain more listening ears when I talk about the interest of others, my imperfections, and less about my dreams. From the media and schools I have learned that people go to therapists in order to be heard. Maybe someday, I will have that experience but being financially challenged that is not a current option for me. As time passed, I have felt sad because I realized I want to be heard more than time allows.

Star Quality on Screen and Holidays

Often we see entertainers hosting holiday events or learn that many stayed home during the holidays. I am not a well-known actress right now but to me, I live as a star actress within. Holidays are hard for me too not just because I want to provide more holiday gifts than I can afford but I want a husband with me. Sure many times I have participated in holiday events but I felt incomplete. I wonder if statistics will show that more entertainers spend time with their families when they are married versus single.

Chapter II

Insecurities of a Star

Attire

I dream of the day I am able to wear all that I like as a star. Sure my budget is an obstacle and not knowing how to make my own clothes but I have done my best to mix and match what I have along with adding accessories in my current situation.

For example, I opened a bank account for second chance people like myself due to my credit all toward getting my finances in order. The program dictated that I make ten purchases a month. So, I chose to buy three clothing items separately twice a month at a convenient store and use the other four qualifying purchases on other bills.

My mother blessed me with a tummy tuck and I definitely look neater in my clothes in the mid-section. Please note only 7 pounds was deducted from my weight with that tummy tuck. It has been two years and I have been able to maintain a size eight for the past year. A solid six is what I would like to be to look neat as I see within.

Fall Back Job, Destiny, or Fear?

Hidden in my soul as a child I wanted all of that attention that stars receive. Yet, I went for the safety net of becoming a teacher because I was good at teaching even as a child and I agree with the cliché that you should not put all of your eggs in one basket. Indeed, being a teacher can display star resilience because a classroom of students is an audience that most often consists of the toughest critics. Part of the package of being a star is being subjected to critics. Certainly, critics can inspire people to improve. When classes are required to perform plays, teachers get a chance to create sets, audition students, direct and coach students during rehearsals. Also teachers get a chance to use a microphone to address adults and hundreds of students like stars.

Nevertheless, I held onto the notion that I could become a teacher as a child because all I would have to do was continue getting good grades in school and continue helping people with learning. Although, I've spent many years as a teacher I have been acting along the way. Destiny will prevail. Shyness has hindered my journey to become the star I have envisioned. At this point, I have planned how my life will look and thrive as a star. Now, it is a matter of time for the star in me to walk into reality with strategic plans that will help people for many years to come.

Voice Vehicle

The first place, I learned to use a microphone was during my first certificated teaching experience in Watts, California. The ambiance of that experience reverberated to the point I was fascinated by its power. Additionally, I learned that even a subtle voice spoken into a microphone could resonate a dynamic impact into the body.

Likewise, I fell in love with the power of the microphone for its intensity to magnify a room.

It would be approximately ten years after my first experience using a microphone that I would perform Stand-Up Comedy. However, I did have a chance to speak on a microphone when I was a child. I have family members that had a band and performed at family gatherings but because I was shy I would not even talk into the microphone.

Undeniably, that exposure planted a seed that I would like to become a singer too. However, singing looked like something I would have to refrain from being shy. Also, I thought I would have to learn how to play instruments because my family members were singers that played various instruments as well.

I was scared. Yes, I let fear thwart my desire to become a singer. In spite of this I gave it a chance as an adult in a karaoke room at a bowling alley. I started off so good that people stood up and clapped for me. I had fun sharing my childhood dream of singing that was displayed by the way I sang the beginning stanzas of a Patti Labelle song. Yes, you know I thought I could sing in my mind since my first choice was a Patti Labelle Song! Unfortunately, I let fear overcome that experience as well. Although the karaoke screen was available for the words I didn't know it didn't matter, my voice went to the left. People didn't understand what happened. I did; I got scared because the adrenaline of exerting a childhood dream subsided in midstream of the song and reality set in that I was actually singing in front of people— *outside of my house.*

Following that experience I attended a workshop for a talent agency where a singer from an academy school would encourage me to sing in front of a room to follow notes played on a piano. Surprisingly, I did okay because by the time my heartbeat slowed down I was already seated back in a chair. Overwhelming, yes, but it was so much fun getting attention with that microphone. In the future, I do plan on taking singing lessons so that I can learn to sing pleasantly throughout whole songs and to perform at places where there is karaoke.

Critic

Currently, I am not a well-known star but I have experienced my first critic. I had the opportunity to work on four commercial sets for a Super-bowl. Unfortunately, neither won but I won the experience after so many auditions. The critic did not believe I had been on a commercial set needless to say four. The website and direct links were supplied and the critic did not say anything else to me for a period of time. Approximately, one month later the same critic approached me to ask when was I going to be on television. I debut on a major network show including the previews of the show a couple of months later. That critic did not say anything about that and millions of people saw the previews because they were shown during commercials of a preceding well-known show. During that timeframe, my feelings were hurt and I did not want to understand the negativity especially since I considered that critic to be my friend.

Chapter III

On-Set Experience

Stage Experience

The audition process for my first theatre gig went like this:

I showed up early and sat in the parking lot away from the entrance of the theatre. Once it was approximately twenty minutes until call time I entered the theatre and wrote my name on the sign-in sheet extremely neat. Then, I sat down with the sides that were provided next to the sign-in sheet. From my novice training prior to going to Miami, Florida for that International Talent Showcase, it was advised that you study your sides, smile to people, and only speak when spoken to in order to keep the voice level down just in case cameras are rolling. There was a great number of talking and children running around in the waiting area. I thought I was in a doctor's office! Skepticism sat in because there I was on my first audition since Miami and it was nothing like I could imagine. Needless to say there would be more audition settings that made me question how can I become a star under these circumstances?

My name was called so I walked around the curtain. There I was, front and center of a table of people encompassing the director, producer, stage managers, and a videographer. I performed two monologues that I performed in Miami. It was a success. So, the next round was to stand in line with other actresses. There were a couple of more actresses that performed their monologues and were either thanked or asked to join the line I was standing in. Then sides were read independently and as scene study. Later that week, I was notified via email that I made the cut and the itinerary of the first rehearsal was included. How was I going to factor in the gas money I was going to need to travel that far? It worked out because I landed a long-term substitute teaching position.

On my first day at rehearsal, I was sitting quite a distance from another actress who was sitting on a couch across from me. I kept trying to figure out why she was frowning at me. The most prevalent thought I kept in the forefront was she might be one of the writers as well as an actress and was wishing I would say her words differently. It didn't occur to me until the next day, that the sole of one of my shoes was loose and it dangled when I crossed my legs. It was indeed embarrassing. No, I did not have money to purchase another pair of shoes prior to the next rehearsal. So what I did was keep my feet on the floor during rehearsal as we sat and read our lines.

On another theatre rehearsal set, I had to endure being fitted and that was embarrassing because most of the dresses were small. That night, I ate pancakes at a 24hr restaurant and stayed up throughout the night drinking free refills of coffee. Then I went to the gym to shower. After work the next day, I visited my grandparents, ate a real meal and slept for a couple of hours. That was my prideful way of overcoming that embarrassment. Nonetheless, I began to spend more time at the gym outside of taking my showers there. I lost twenty pounds during the course of that theatre run and would later gain it back.

It was after another theatre run that a newspaper printed a review of the show stating, I could not find the light. What! When you are told where your mark will be and is rehearsed and performed time after time that is what you are to do. The pain felt from that experience was nothing like my first critic experience. In fact, I rationalized it as a learning experience that if lighting becomes an issue it is okay to make a slight adjustment. It was a different person working the lights that night of all nights when the newspaper writer was there. In hindsight, this experience planted a seed toward my company, Journey to Stardom Productions. Currently, I still need lighting equipment. Additionally in hindsight, I am elated that my first newspaper debut from a different theatre run was one of favor. I made front page of a newspaper along with the cast in Torrance, California.

Theatre Stench

Another stage experience consisted of a stench in an office building that was so sour my nose eventually ignored the stench so that I could concentrate on the rehearsal. Likewise, the other actors and actresses must have been just as passionate about building acting resumes that we didn't talk about the stench. The stench came from the director's laundry that he washed and air-dried in the back room. It would later be known that the space was not in building code compliance for theatrical performances and he would no longer be able to stage plays there. Aside of the stench, I would have loved to live in my own office space, wrote, directed, and put on plays. Based on my circumstances at that time I understood his journey. That director is one of a few that has helped to inspire me to create my own company, Journey to Stardom Productions.

Embarrassing Stench in a Theatre

Then there was a time I endured a stench for eight weeks on my journey to stardom. First of all, the stage manager who always wore tank tops even when it was freezing cold became the director. It was great to see someone receive a promotion in the industry. Nonetheless, the stench that was evident in this theatre did not come from laundry. During this theatre run I tried to understand why the director smelled so much. You never know what the next person may be enduring. An actor that could not take it anymore talked to the director on a personal level. The director apologized to the cast and informed us of his living situation and also explained that the bumps on his arms and neck were from bed bugs. Just to think, I thought the frogs and lizards were a bit much to encounter as I walked back and forth from my hotel room on that beautiful terrain to perform for various divisions at that International Talent Showcase in Miami.

Theatre and Stand-Up Comedy

My favorite style of performance in a theatre is stand-up comedy. There are various styles of comedy. Some people use profanity others do not. Some comedians focus on one genre maybe spirituality or entertainers. The list goes on. My current and past perspective is it provides an outlet to say things that do not consist of proper English and what many families hear at family gatherings and would not be professional at a workplace. I enjoy the freedom to walk back and forth across stage to get that instantaneous gratification. When plays are performed most often the audience applauds at the end of each scene and you may have walked off stage already. Who are they really clapping for? Indeed, applause are given for the ensemble and all of the hands that it takes to produce a successful play but honestly come on every actress and actor wants individual recognition each time they work as well. Stand-Up Comedy is awesome and that is why I think actors/actresses also perform Stand-Up Comedy because most often actors/actresses work on closed sets versus live sets.

Filming in the Woods

It was a painful experience. I was provided a big momma like suit that was not adequately stuffed with proper padding. From the top of a staircase I was to begin with a scoot and slide downstairs and demonstrate over the top excitement about seeing a character that was already sitting on the bottom step. I did that over and over again because the director thought it was funny. A cameraman told the director the film could be replayed and that the daylight was being expended. Live entertainment is different than rewinding film. At any rate, by the time that day was over and the adrenaline had subsided my hip hurt so badly, I could barely walk. Not long before that filming experience, my grandmother had a hip replacement. She was able to provide me with an over the counter topical cream that would decrease the pain and she gave me a cane that would assist me with stepping up and down curbs and to get in and out of my car.

Unfortunately, this film has not been published to my knowledge because the director and the editor had ill words on set. The editor left to no return. The director explained that a court date would be set and to this day I don't know if that actually occurred. Nonetheless, months later that director asked if I would be willing to film that movie again with a different editor on set. No, I did not. Not only did I get hurt, it was the negative aura about the set that I did not want to experience again. For example, people complained about the fees for the food and cabins. In addition, many people complained about how the director directed. They really felt bad about how much I was directed to slide downstairs to the point the cameraman said he refused to continue filming because he did not want to stand by and watch me hurt myself. Another person during that situation shared with someone else in a very strong voice that I deserved a purple heart for my effort at trying to follow the director's directions.

Indeed my work ethic is off the charts. Moreover my heart was captivated by all of that attention from the team of people on set and I did not want to stop the film because I was hurt. By the way, the Laker fan in me stepped up to the line at that time and like Kobe Bryant has modeled, great players get hurt but they don't want to stop playing the game. Acting is playing to me because I love it just that much. However I did learn the physical interpretation of the cliché –don't let it get the best of you. I knew my hip was beginning to hurt but not to the extreme that it would hurt the next day. In addition, that was an extremely long ride home after the many days of filming because I was driving a stick-shift car with excruciating pain in my hip.

Film Festival

A director called me from a scene study audition I didn't think went as well for me as the actress playing the other part. A prime example, that you never know what a director is looking for or when you are too over-the-top. It turns out that although the lady had snatched her wig off during the scene and was hilarious it did not land her the part. The director informed me it was my responsiveness to the improv that kept the scene going that impressed him. After this audition, I would be successful with wig humor at the Normandie Casino. A casino where many people may remember Cedric the Entertainer hosted a named comedy show. It is amazing how dots are connected when you are on a journey to stardom.

Hmmm... When I was at that International Talent Showcase, I saw a gentleman lean toward my soon to be agent when my scene study partner skipped a line and I responded with words that carried the scene. So, I have learned and gleaned from a director who won acknowledgement in a Film Festival, knowing how to carry lines is a worthy skill.

Filming at a Renown Film Academy in Burbank, California

Aw wow! Imagine walking into a movie theatre and you see all of those poster board props of stars and walls covered with posters of movies in picture frames. Then narrow the width of that space when you walk into a movie theatre to a hallway in a house. The audition and the day of filming both felt the same to me. Although I would be filming an exercise scene, I felt like I was walking down the path of an Escalade limousine to approach a red carpet event. Affirmative, I was walking tall, courageous, and full of ambition.

Unfortunately, I did not maintain that affective aura when a few weeks later, I would attend an A-list audition a few buildings away. I was out of my league at that time!

Chapter IV

A-List Audition

My agent called me about an audition for a Martin Lawrence movie. Yes! Who knows which movie because what I have learned auditions can be placebos for other movies than the one you think. Before I opened the door to the office, I felt a force of wealth. I did not know how to receive it at that time. All of the women were wearing a puffy hairstyle including me but I recognized their faces from television. The waiting room setting was beautiful. I listened to a receptionist make an arrangement for a tour bus and my imagination took off when I should have been in deep focus embracing the sides so that I would land the job.

When it was my turn to go into another room where there was a panel of three people. I was overwhelmed and out of my element. When I entered the room for the audition, I was not ready. Indeed, you need to be ready so that you don't have to get ready. I did not slate strong or connect immediately with fervent emotions. I would later learn how to invoke fervent emotions with immediacy from acting classes in Santa Monica, California. When it was time for me to leave, I couldn't even get out of the door. I just wanted to start over. The man from the panel came around the table to open the door so I could get out of there. In the effort of saving face, I began some poor example of a boogie role, also a role that I would need to rehearse especially when it was just the week before that I was scooping cat poop in lieu of sleeping in my car. What happened at the audition?

All I can do now is wish that audition tape will become available to me. From listening to interviews even named stars can recall auditions that could have been better. It just pains me until this day that my most prestigious audition and opportunity to perform on a Martin Lawrence movie was one I performed the worst to date. In contrast, it could possibly still become a clip on a blooper reel on a major network in the world of dreams.

Beyond that there was a man that looked so much like Martin Lawrence who walked down the hallway just before my name was called. Wait a minute was that him in real-life? It was too much excitement for me at the time. That is a statement and not an excuse. Additionally, at that time, I had not yet experienced being a stand-up comedienne in a nightclub. I needed to know how to turn awe from being in the company of other comediennes in a snap to the grandeur that I am a star too, people just don't know it yet. Be that as it may, I am looking forward to another opportunity to audition and land a principal part in a Martin Lawrence movie.

The Wildest Audition So far

After a dry spell of landing parts from many auditions, I decided the next audition I was going to take out my energy in whatever the next part would be to make myself feel better about the fact that I have so much to give. It really wasn't going to matter if I got the part or not but I was going to be in control of what I was going to give and I was just going to use the audition as a stage. My game face was on like a champion swimmer who has their gear and goggles on and their stature demonstrates they know how to take care of business in the swimming pool.

So, I put my wig on and started the engine in my car. I drove with a pensive attitude that I will be recognized for my acting skills today and it will be no questions. Once I was inside the very small room, I used it as if I was on a stage of a 1500 seat theatre. There were two people sitting behind a desk, the kind you see in classrooms and there was one person standing behind a tripod with a camera. The direction was to act out the slide however I wanted and with the wildest interpretation I could perform. Excellent! Just the permission I needed. So, I gave them the lioness in me for sounds. I took my shoes off and hopped around almost up and down the walls even with my dress and stockings. I was so wild with my antics I tore my stockings, pulled at my wig that was locked down—not easily accessible to pull off, and I moved around with so much energy I scared the cameraman. It was funny and scary for all of them. Surely, I did what I set out to do which was to expel my energy and let people know that I had more to give than a nice smile and good reading skills. After walking out of that audition room I was certain I wouldn't get that part especially since I scared the cameraman, nonetheless, I did get the part.

Auditioning

Auditions are a mystery to me because soon as I think for certain I didn't land a part, sometimes that is the one I get. At other times, I felt so good about the audition that sometimes I would get the part and moreover I would not get the part. Based on my many auditioning experiences, the ones I had the most fun with they all became my characters. So, I can only encourage people to do what you feel moreover than what you think the people in the audition room expect based on the sides.

Also, when I was hitting the pavement hard, broke and all, I couldn't see beyond the trees regarding how I was landing certain parts versus other ones that I wanted just as much. Another good lesson, I learned from my acting class in Santa Monica, California under the direction of Brooklyn McLinn was to journal my experiences from auditions and other experiences in the entertainment industry. After gaining that

information, I landed two parts back to
back. Yes! I had a repeat for the first time.

As I recollect my entertainment experiences in
California while sitting in my living room in Las
Vegas, Nevada, I await the time I can afford to
begin the auditioning process in Hollywood,
California again. Similarly, I remember the
emotions I'm feeling right now because there was
an audition whereas it seemed certain I had the
part as a bailiff. A question presented itself about
whether or not I would be willing to travel to
San Diego, California to say a couple of sentences
and I was standing in Hollywood, California in front
of two directors and one of them was behind a
camera with a huge lens, he was Lou Diamond Jr. If
I would have been a principle actress---had more
lines they would have possibly paid my expenses
even though it was a new production company.
Unfortunately at that time, it would have caused a
hardship to pay my own expenses to say a couple
of lines on a movie. Yet a couple of lines is a big
deal because a couple of lines can help you reach
stardom and certainly a couple of lines here and
there multiplied by the amount those lines are
replayed by many people. For example, people
have put a couple of lines together and some action
on You-tube and became stars.

Time, money, memory, attire, and
transportation, are just a handful of details that are
taken into account when preparing to audition. I
encourage you to get prepared with basic

necessities and prepare for alternatives for example bring a lunch just in case the audition is not catered and you have a couple of hours to drive or catch the bus home, or you're not there long enough to stay for a food break. The process of preparation before an audition, during, and after is a job before you land a job. Auditions are an investment in yourself because it is education and on the job training all in one for the career you want.

Audition for International Talent Showcase

It was five years ago when I auditioned for my first acting class. It was held at the Palace Station Hotel in Las Vegas, Nevada in preparation for that International Talent Showcase. I performed in nine divisions successfully: TV Commercial, Soap-Opera, Cold Read, Scene Study, Monologue, Creative Runway, Spokesperson, Close-Up, and Stand-Up Comedy. In Miami, I performed in front of my largest live audience thus far. After approximately four years, I would build a varied acting resume and begin my company, Journey To Stardom Productions. Next I would walk away from a teaching position because of lack of support and full of pride, which would cease my auditioning process because of lack of money. Undeniably, it takes money to audition. Auditioning is a job where you pay yourself 100% until someone else gives you a promotion and they begin to pay you a nominal fee. Similarly, many parts are not paid but you are always paid in experience.

Can you help me with financial aid for Auditioning?

Many people have asked me about auditions, the characters I played, how much money I've made and much more. The most intriguing question centers around money. I wish there was financial aid for auditioning. It could work whereas a timeline of five years would be granted. If within that timeframe, a gig is acquired and would pay for the five year financial aid the actor/actress would be required to pay off the balance. If after five years the actor/actress does not land a high paying gig, then the actor/actress would have to begin paying 25% of their net pay from their day job. At any point during the five years, the actor/actress would be able to cancel the financial aid award and begin paying 20% of their net pay from their day job. Nonetheless, when I become a star, I plan to gain assistance with building a financial aid business plan for the purpose of helping others with the auditioning process.

Parking Ticket Audition

On this audition, I parked at a meter that already had approximately one hour left. The audition notice stated the timeframe and provided information about the importance of arriving on time and if not on time you would be turned away and that parking will be a challenge. The information that was not supplied was that the waiting room would be full and once you entered the room for the audition it may take longer than expected if they think you may be selected for the television show. Yes, I received a parking ticket. I landed the part and I have yet to see myself on the show but friends and family have seen me more than once on that television show. The money I was paid from that show was $3 short of the money I had to pay for the parking ticket. Yes, I continued to audition after that and honestly with a little reluctance. The next audition would be shadowed with the worry that I may receive another parking ticket because there weren't any parking signs on the street. No, I did not receive another parking ticket or land that part but following that audition, I did land a part for another television show. Keep trying!

Most Dangerous Television Set

The audition for this particular television show would pay $50,000 to the first place contestant. It called for dangerous attempts on land, water, and in the air. The acts were so dangerous each contestant had to sign a contract that included waiving the right to sue if injuries or death occurred. Also, each contestant was sent to a doctor for a physical to ensure no heart attacks or the like would occur on set. One of the questions at the doctor's office was do you need the money that bad, you are willing to risk your life?

Well, I wasn't looking at the ordeal in that manner although I had already read and signed the contract. The star in me was elated about being on television. I told the doctor, yes, I do need the money badly but I also believe God will protect me. No, I did not win first place but I won a lot of air-time. The preview of this show was shown for a couple of weeks. Best of all, my youngest daughter called me from her grandparents house and told me, Mommy, I see you on TV! To receive that call from my daughter about my first appearance on a historical major network will stand as one of many thrills in my life. I filmed myself watching that preview at my apartment in Hawthorne, California.

Furthest and Closest Television Set

When you're short of cash, it's common to think about how much gas money will be involved when you have to drive to the various filming locations. It was four days in total to complete this project and it worked out that on the last day of filming, the location was about fifteen minutes away and I was on my last quarter of a tank of gas. It all worked out and it was so much fun pretending to be in a different country. Likewise, the feeling of walking through the masses of people while being filmed was so exciting; I wanted other people to enjoy that experience. So, I began auditioning people at a music studio for my company Journey to Stardom Productions. Thereafter, I filmed actors/actresses at other places and I'm still in progress of developing this company.

Family and Friends on Film

It was a rewarding experience to be contacted by a producer of a film that learned of me from an audition reel from a friend. Yes, I did ask from which audition did he learn of me but he said it was confidential. Subsequently, I learned that it is possible that you can still land a part from simply being on audition reels. Furthermore, this producer allowed me to invite my family and friends to act on set. It was so much fun to be able to give my family and friends an opportunity to experience being on set. One of those family members would later bring his friends to my apartment to write and film a short film for my production company. That film is in the process of being edited.

Chapter V

Background Work

My cousins that operate Comedy Show venues motivated me to try background work considering the fact that I was between jobs and had a car. Nevertheless, people without cars were doing background work too. I know because I dropped many of them off at bus and train stops. Later, I would pick some of them up so that they could write, perform, and direct for my company, Journey to Stardom Productions.

Based on the amount of background work I have done, I have not seen myself in the background on any of the shows I worked. Nonetheless, I did get the paychecks for all of the work and free food while on set. In contrast, when watching television, I have seen sets I have worked on and can place where I stood or what was moved to make the set more appropriate to different shows.

It is a trip that I did not begin my journey to stardom with background work because I really enjoy learning and planning as much as possible about a subject before I teach or perform the lesson. Passion for something will supersede typical logic at times. Overall, my experience with background work has been fun, exciting, and informative. The experience of being on different sets with people that had good attitudes and upcoming comedians were a lot of fun. It was exciting to see stars and watch film crews work. Film crews are a group of intricate stars because they produce the outcome of collective creativity from writers, directors....

Additionally the scenery of being on set at various studios and locations enlightened my perception of what is seen on television from learning how scenes are filmed. For example, I learned from sitting amongst a crowd at the Santa Anita Racetrack Park, the editor would eventually add additional sections of audiences based on frames from the live audience in order to provide the appearance that the stadium was packed.

That particular film crew as well acted as teachers because they took the time to explain to the actors and actresses why they were going to have us stand, sit, and walk encompassing the pacing needed for various scenes.

On this set I said hello to Dustin Hoffman and he said hello with his wonderful smile. In addition, the food was set up like a venue at a hotel in Las Vegas, Nevada. The servers wore uniforms, sliced meat, spooned vegetables, scooped ice cream, and so much more. Furthermore, people could go back for more food and beverages.

In contrast, the most painful experience I endured from background work was from having the individual eyelashes removed inside the hair and make-up trailer that I just had done the evening before. Yes, that was excruciating pain and I felt like I looked like a plucked chicken while I waited to be called to do crosses on set.

The most uncomfortable feeling from doing background work was acknowledging flirtation from an ex-boyfriend of a family member. At first, it was nice to see him and to learn that he was interested in becoming an actor. In addition, it was nice to learn for the first time of a person that was in the medical field wanted to become a star too, yet waited after retirement to begin the journey to stardom. Many people do begin with background work on the journey to stardom because it is widely suggested due to how much you will learn from being on sets. For example, you will learn from listening to the notes given to the stars from the directors.

Most often there is a person in charge of directing the background actors so that there isn't any confusion about how many times an actor or actress crossed the camera on various scenes. For example, I crossed in front of an A-list star, Dustin Hoffman. When another scene was being filmed a different background director called me over to pretend to be a photographer on the grass as the horses pranced around. I love horses so it would not have been a challenge for me to be really close to them. Nonetheless because I crossed in front of a star, Dustin Hoffman, which is called a prominent cross, I was not able to act as a photographer in the scene with the horses. Instead of being filmed so close to those horses I was able to stand in the front row of the other actors and actresses by the white fence surrounding the horses. At any rate that was the time I learned about prominent crosses from background work.

In contrast, the most embarrassing experience from background work was hearing another actress tell a group of people that I didn't know the reason why my boots were sounding like Captain Hook. It was because the silver part protruded from the inside of my left boot.

A novelty experience from doing background work was after I exchanged greetings with Steve Harris who had a great sense of humor on set. Wilmer Valderrama approached me while I was standing in a police uniform to tell me that I looked so much like one of his good friends. He was referring to, Regina King. He shared at length how amazing that I looked so much like her that I could be her sister. I enjoyed the conversation and the attention. Unaware to him, I have been told that I look like Regina King ever since she played a daughter on the show, 227. I really wanted to be called to do background on the show, Southland, so I could meet her since it seems like I've been living in her shadow practically all of my life.

Just a note: When Regina King was on the front cover of a magazine in 2006, I was a fourth grade teacher. There was a student that was in the first grade who asked me if I was the lady on the magazine at the grocery store as he walked passed me in his class line. That was a precious experience and again in 2012, Wilmer Valderrama excitedly shares the similarities of our appearances.

Long-term Background Work as a Police Officer

In essence, the experience of observing prevalent television and movie actors at work has been instrumental to the development of the star I will become. For example, when you see stars walking around going over their lines as they walk around the set before cameras roll, they seem to care less about how people perceive them while talking to themselves. Another example is the joy that many stars share while communicating with other actors, make-up artists, and other people while waiting for the camera crew to reset in preparation for the next scene. In addition, as the stars performed, they appeared to be sincerely relaxed as if the lines were what they would actually say in a conversation off set. Background work is indeed similar to an acting class however you don't have to pay for the class; they pay you.

Chapter VI

Acting Classes

Roger Thomas from the What's Happening Show was my first acting coach when I was a child. I learned that it does not pay to be shy because people don't have time to draw energy or information out of you. Likewise, from what I've learned thus far, the industry wants people to be ready for action and would prefer if the actor/actress would be over the top because it is easier to calm a person down than to encourage someone to project the ambiance of a character that is extremely upset or happy. Another lesson, I learned if I were not confident in myself other people would not have confidence in me that I can perform. For example, I was overweight and shy. I didn't want to take my coat off because I looked like I weighed more than everyone else in the room. Also, that experience planted a seed in my mind that if I'm not willing to take off a coat which will allow me to be more comfortable to perform how could I be ready to perform when it's hot.

In addition, I learned to project energy that I was ready to perform and confident in my own skin. That skill would later propel me to be chosen time and time again out of standing lines. For example, my next acting classes would be called drama classes. In each class, I would be selected out of lines or rows of student desks to do improv as examples for other students who were new to performing or were shy. From that childhood experience at Roger Thomas's acting class in Compton, California, I have been able to become successful at being an icebreaker at other acting classes as an adult, meetings, conferences, and exude more confidence as an actress.

Drama Class at a University

The initial purpose of taking this class was to satisfy a requirement toward my California teaching credential. Once, the first day of class was over, I would walk to the bus stop. On the bus, I daydreamed of being a star. First of all, I envisioned a large audience clapping for me and my smile would be so big my cheeks would hurt. It felt so real. Although it would be approximately five years later that my first audience would be the largest audience yet and I can remember my cheeks did hurt from smiling so big. The power of the imagination is amazing. Also, I daydreamed about the car I would drive considering I didn't have a working car at the time. I envisioned a silver Mercedez Benz. I still want a silver Mercedez Benz.

At any rate, I received an "A" from that drama class because I walked in and out of the class as if I was already a star yet with a humble spirit. Also, during the class time, I was on the edge of my seat listening and always eager to perform and even teach the class. My classmates shared their joy every time I performed. The professor suggested that I audition for parts at the campus's theatre and take more classes in performing arts. What happened?

My left-brain took over because it was a safe route to obtain a college degree and become a teacher. That semester, I was taking too many classes, catching the bus, and working full-time, yes I used those circumstances to prevent me to attend my first audition. I didn't think about planning for the next semester whereas I could have incorporated performing arts classes and stayed to course on my timeframe I planned for acquiring the teaching credential considering I had learned to successfully carry more than six classes per semester. Parallel to that, I was afraid that I might change my major at a time that I was very close to completing that degree. Nevertheless, yes, I wish I had taken more performing arts classes. Indeed, it is not too late.

In addition, due to the various drama lessons learned in that class, it exemplifies how teachers can inspire students to dream and encourage students to expound on qualities that will help other people. For example, when I become a star, I will be able to help other people dream, learn and heal by acting as various characters, provide monetary investments, and give motivational speeches just as other stars have done.

Worldwide Star Search

It wasn't too long after I completed the above drama class that I applied for the Worldwide Star Search. I consider this experience a class versus an audition because I paid money to participate. Do not pay for auditions because there isn't a guarantee you will land the part anyway. At any rate, the first task was to see if I was photogenic. I was instructed to make as many faces as possible while a camera took many pictures. While I waited to be seen by an acting coach I observed other people across the band of age groups studying little pieces of paper. At that time, I didn't know those were called, sides. People were practicing to audition for commercials.

Once, I was summoned into an office, it turned out to be an interview about why I wanted to become a star and about the money entailed to continue the process. It wasn't long after I became a certificated teacher so I had the money to continue the process but on a payment plan. The next task on a different day was to participate in a workshop with a room full of people from teens to seniors. We stood in a shape of a crescent moon for a couple of hours. I don't even remember having to stand that long in my life at that time.

I definitely know the difference between a sedentary lifestyle and an active lifestyle now but at that time I don't think the word sedentary was even in my vocabulary. So, I learned the need for stamina in the entertainment industry. I did begin to stand more even at home when I watched television. From that experience, I became more cognizant of my posture as well. Furthermore, when I would later go on auditions that did consist of standing in long lines for long periods of time it did not make me fret because I was conditioned for the endurance needed.

The workshop was comprised of learning how to walk with power, give affirmative handshakes, use sides for commercials to practice projecting our voices, and to prepare for a close-up interview. That was when I learned that interviews and auditions were similar if not one and the same.

Literally, various people of the team stood a foot away from your face and asked about your purpose for becoming a star. Then we were put in pairs and to interview each other. Afterwards we reported to the whole group about what we remembered about the information provided from the person we interviewed encompassing whether or not they were nervous, confident, or shy.

During that experience I practiced active listening, something I learned from a speech class I took in school and that was how I was able to remember a heightened number of details about what the person I interviewed shared.

Also, from this experience I learned that I knew how to react naturally to another character because when I could hear the gentlemen sound as if he was nervous, I asked about how much he was enjoying the workshop for the purpose of redirecting his nervous energy to the possible circumstance that unnerved him. Certainly, as he answered the questions the nervousness in his voice dissipated because he addressed how he was feeling at that moment and possibly subconsciously realized there wasn't a reason for him to be nervous because we were all there learning and had paid to be there.

After a couple of more workshops like the one above there were others that were comprised of classifying your acting style. For example, I am a commercial actress because I'm over the top and love to smile. However, I can do a repertoire of characters and genres. In addition, we rehearsed walking on a runway, pretending to audition for a commercial, and interviews for a talent agent.

Thereafter, I participated in the Commercial Women's Division. I had my aunt Cathie put a weave in my hair and it was off the chain! I had been drinking a lot of water so my skin was beautiful. Also, I had been exercising and actually had lost ten pounds before the event so I was feeling and looking good. Moreover, I took into account the lessons learned from the workshop, walked the runway like I was the most beautiful woman there even with my two stomachs, had the two commercials memorized, and owned the stage like everybody was there just to see me complete a goal. At the end of the day, it was so exciting to see my face appear on that large screen as the first place winner for that division.

That was also another time I was alone receiving recognition for something so fantastic towards my journey to stardom. I cry as I reflect because it was so nice just to hear the thunder of applause. It was a reward for the sacrifices I made to be there and my effort toward being the best actress I knew how. Nevertheless, being there alone has added to my character as well as a testimony that at times you may have to stand alone to get things done. Nonetheless, I did have support but my pride wouldn't allow me to ask my parents, grandparents, or a friend to attend the event with me especially considering I didn't have the finances to pay for additional tickets for them to attend.

In hindsight, I walked away from that event with an extraordinary experience as well as a winner so the tears are a reflection of rewarded repressed perseverance and joy. After the winners were announced there was an opportunity to attend a close-up interview with a director that was scheduled to direct a film in Oregon. That is the time I learned that directors make character selections. Mr. Fox was such a nice man and he was dressed to the tee! I remember being conscientious about my bottom stomach sitting on my lap and noticeable because I had to wear a plain colored blouse and I didn't have any spanks so all of my rolls were prevalent. By this time, I was aware of the need to dress comfortably as well as appropriately according to venues. So, I wish my blouse had a collar to project at least an allure of being in better physical shape.

Once I had the opportunity to sit in front of Mr. Fox, I exuded as much confidence as I could and it didn't take that much because I just won a first place blue ribbon. At any rate, after the greetings, he disclosed the energy that would be needed to perform the scenes. He also shared his concern of whether or not I would be able to meet those demands of the scene he described. I was hungry to be an actress so I pushed up my right short sleeve and showed him my muscle but I had not exercised my triceps. Even the people in the line waiting to interview with him laughed. Then he asked me if I could cry on cue. My mind was like what? In that instance he reworded the question because he could see I had no clue of what I was suppose to do. So, I tried to cry but I can only imagine I must have looked like I was trying to force out a reluctant bowel movement and the onlookers were laughing. In addition, I had the nerve to ask him if he could see that my eyes were wet. He said I was his best interview yet but he could not offer me the part. Furthermore, he suggested that I get into an acting class and learn more about the business.

Overall, the experience with the Worldwide Star Search was highly engaging, inspiring, fun, and informative. Additionally, after this experience the principal at the elementary school in California I was working for allowed me to share my experience during the morning assembly following the weekend I participated in the Worldwide Star Search event. The purpose was to practice becoming a motivational speaker for students as a star. Moreover to exemplify courage to pursue dreams while working another job is possible.

Acting Class in Santa Monica, California

When I arrived it felt like an audition. The class was held in a theatre. The other actors/actresses observed me as if the class was a competition. Somewhere in my life, I learned that it is possible to change the dynamics in a room. So, I decided to sit above the other classmates so that I would be able to observe them from a distance. After a couple of weeks, I was asked to sit closer to the other students. Needless to say, I was able to take better notes when I sat away from the gossiping but I did gain from the experience how some critics may work. For example, when the classmates that worked like critics had their turn on stage it was apparent that they surveyed the class to see if any gossiping was going on. I had a lot of fun watching the dynamics of the class just as they may have got a kick out of observing me as a classmate.

One of the most challenging lessons in this class was to study our past in order to build a repertoire of readily emotions. For example, I had to list a number of events in my life that were emotionally charged by feelings of sadness, anger, embarrassment, and joy. Then, I had to study the events under the scope of how I felt during and after the event as well as facial expressions and or reactions of people involved. Thereafter, the class was instructed to revisit our notes from time to time to keep those feelings charged versus repressed. Ultimately the lesson's objective was to teach actors and actresses how to draw upon feelings from real experiences that can be fueled into emotions of characters instantly.

The following experience is an example of a highly emotional stage in my life where I was able to pull various feelings from to work with during this lesson in my acting class in Santa Monica, California:

In my early twenties, I lay in a hospital in Las Vegas, Nevada. In the midst of a doctor's visit before I knew it there was blood spewed everywhere from the floor to the ceiling and all I could hear was screaming. A tumor was punctured inside my uterus. At this time in my life, I was gaining momentum of being independent and my pride was evident. I did all of the blood work and xrays before the surgery in preparation to remove the tumor before I called my parents. To fathom how much audacity I had to conceal a surgery, my first surgery from my parents who love me so much even to this day. I am still harboring pain from how much I hurt them from not giving them the opportunity to be there initially for their oldest child at a horrific time.

My mother happened to work at that very hospital and it was one of her co-workers that called her to let her know I was losing blood to a devastating degree that I had a blood transfusion. My mother is a very strong woman but I can only imagine how much strength she had to muster up as she listened to the information provided to her. Of all days, she had friends and family over for a party. She just called me the night before to inquire about my work schedule to see if I would be able to attend. My schedule did not permit my attendance.

When I woke up from the surgery, my mother was to my immediate right and family was surrounding my bed. I was in trouble with the boss, my mother. They had to ask her to leave the recovery room. At that time, she was in one of those cycles of dealing with pain. I had scared her so much that she displayed she was upset maybe in all actuality angry. Without telling my mother about my scheduled surgery and receiving that call from her co-worker was an embarrassment to her and communicated the outlandish pride of mine.

My mother and family members remained in the waiting room to wait for the outcome of the tumor. One of those aunts would soon die of lung cancer. In the meantime, I was moved from the recovery room to the cancer ward. While I was in the room, I slept and slept because I was scared to be awake, awaiting bad news. Also, I was in shock. Nobody told me that I was going to lie in a cancer ward after the surgery. I thought I would return home to my apartment to heal and go back to work.

A nurse let me know that a team of people would arrive shortly to tell me the results of tests that were done on the tumor that was removed. Well, that was one audience I did not plan on. Many of the people that were with the doctor were interns experiencing how a doctor tells a patient about the outcome of a tumor. I was blessed to learn that the tumor was benign. Radiation and moreover chemotherapy was what I endured to rid the rest of the tumorous tissues.

After the team left, I cried because of the unknown. Will I lose my hair or die? It was in the midst of crying when I looked out the hospital window with eyes blurred by tears that I envisioned something that looked like a swarm of fireflies coming to me. Immediately after I was quickly trying to clear my eyes, I felt someone sit on my bed and the blanket had an appearance that someone had already sat there. My next thought went to thinking of my father's mother, we called, Grandmother, her name was Thelma. She died of cancer. Even to this day, I believe it was her, Grandmother. She told me not to worry because I have a lot to do and that I was going to be okay. My nerves in my left arm felt as if they were touched. My grandmother was very sweet. Another reason why I believe it was her because one day when I was younger, I sat in my grandfather, Doug-out-Doug's chair across from my grandmother while watching television but she was not watching television she was watching me. When I looked at her, she told me she liked how I sat up in the chair. I was slouching and I corrected myself and she noticed. That one to one special moment in a room by ourselves is the same feeling I felt in that lonely hospital room continues to make me feel adamant about the fact that spirit was of my Grandmother, Thelma.

Once I was able to go home, I called my father and his wife who lived out of state and talked to them about my ordeal. They drove across state seem like in a flash. They brought me food and lots of love. They wanted to take care of me so much especially since I couldn't work at that time and pay my own rent that I began to stay with them and travel back and forth to Nevada from California for chemotherapy treatments weekly even while my father suffered from a sleeping disorder.

Did I lose my hair? No, I did not lose my hair but I lost the layer of skin off of my lips. Imagine a hot link being peeled and the palpable meat protruding and oozing with its liquid yellow fat. My lips burned. Whenever I accidentally pressed my lips together out of habit they would become stuck and would hurt tremendously. My food was pureed and I used a straw whereas I used more of my teeth and a glass to consume food. My favorite was chili beans and cheese until the chemotherapy caused my mouth to become exceptionally sensitive. One day, I was so excited and thanked my mother for buying me my favorite tropical juice that was mixed with mangos, pineapples, etc.... That juice burned my mouth so much, it was then that I learned the phrase, excruciating pain! My mother felt so bad for me, tears formed in her eyes. Tears were already in my eyes. We cried together.

During the time I was enduring chemotherapy to rid the remaining cancerous cells in my uterus, my wedding day was aggressively approaching. The groom was in the military at that time and the hospital bills were paid. To conclude my experience with chemotherapy the doctors informed me that my t-counts increased progressively and I healed at an expedient rate after having been told initially that I may not be able to have children. When my cousin, Cherise learned of this devastating news she adamantly let me know that she would carry a baby for me. Oh so precious! She later gave birth to four more children, may have some more, and is a wonderful grandmother too. Just a note, she must have listened to a lot of Richard Pryor records because when you go to her house you would think you're at a live comedy show held at the Nokia Theatre in California. She is a star comedian in my book.

Unfortunately, I did not listen to the spirit that told me something was wrong when the groom was more worried about getting a part for his car before the store closed while a church full of people were waiting for us to be married. I could hardly talk with the chemotherapy lips. At that time, I hadn't had my first cell phone to call the wedding off or the guts to cancel the hard work and money my father and his wife provided for my wedding. Pride stepped in and put my courage to the side. I can only imagine what it would feel like to be hog-tied in the passenger seat of a car but that is the best example I can provide at this time even after all of these years how I felt waiting for the groom to bring his person out of that parts store. Nonetheless, the manner in which the marriage began is the manner in which it ended because something other than our relationship frequently received more precedence. In less than a year the marriage was over and I later learned that he asked to marry me on a bet. I have lived in Las Vegas, Nevada a couple of periods of my life and with that harboring pain it has deterred me from becoming a gambler.

Toward the end of my chemotherapy treatments, a nurse gave me an artifact made in the likeness of an angel because she said she had never met a patient that received chemotherapy

treatment with as much grace as I displayed.
Well, I had a slight relapse with my lips whereas a scab had developed on my top lip and somehow began to slide to my lower lip and it was pulling on my top lip that hurt so bad my blood pressure went up and I was re-hospitalized. It was two days before I was to be married. The day before, I requested discharge papers. The next morning it was still a challenge to be discharged. At that point I started pulling out the tubes and getting dressed and was not in the mood to hear what I could not do. I was discharged and married the next day.

The above period of my life was filled with so much intensity and a wide range of feelings that it was the best period of my life to study during that acting class in Santa Monica, California. Consequently, that lesson study has definitely improved me as an actress.

Does it take heart to become a star? Yes, I believe so! Similarly, writing a book takes heart with a goal of reaching at least one million people who want to be stars, people that wonder what the first steps of a star's journey were, and many more people for their reasons unknown to me at this time.

There was a time that I sat on a bus stop after being married because the husband had to return to duty and my car was broke. I still used the miniature veil my Aunt Betty made me to cover the chemotherapy lips. I remember talking to the cells in my body about getting better because I want to be a television star and even while I sat on that bench on Charleston in Las Vegas, Nevada I made myself laugh internally about the fact that I can barely talk and I still want to be a star. In order for me to talk I had to talk without permitting my lips to touch. Well there are many words with letters that cause your lips to touch especially words with m's. My light-hearted spirit was curtailed when I got on the bus because a piece of a scab from my bottom lip slid off to my blouse. Oh yeah that was gross and highly embarrassing. Most importantly, imagine I just talked to my cells about healing. Although my dream of becoming a star hasn't happened as fast as me committing my body to healing, the intense feelings from that experience will be vital when I have to portray a character that is embarrassed.

Another Acting Class Experience

It was a trip to work with a scene partner who called to tell me that it was all about me as if it was some type of hierarchy situation. Wow! It was to be a scene not someone coaching me to perform a monologue. From this experience, I learned that there might be other actresses that think just because they have been amongst more key players in the industry than others their attitude will reflect that. Furthermore, that experience reminded me about being humble is more appealing than being arrogant.

Likewise, it was a classmate that shared how intriguing it was to hear about my auditions and parts I landed during our introduction time. I was informed as well that I shared my various experiences with care and how I wanted to help people as a future star. Fundamentally, I shared the information because the acting coach wanted the actors and actresses to share their experiences in the industry before we began our lessons. It was also a time for us to study experiences so that we could all become informed and better with the auditioning process. During that class I was able to inspire a classmate to audition who had attended that class for over a year. I shared my experience of being scared to audition at that university and how I've wanted to be on television since I was in elementary school. In addition, I shared information about an audition opportunity and that I promised to be there and I was there. People that are older than you sometimes need just as much encouragement to complete a task than young people.

In contrast, some people do not need any encouragement to audition, rehearse, or attend acting classes. Likewise, asking questions is okay during an acting class however when asking questions incites negative overtone it is not okay. There was a time during that acting class I did not agree with my acting coach and instead of being quiet I channeled the art of questioning to attempt to sway my perspective as ideal. That did not go over well. It was an embarrassment to the acting coach as well as myself. There were people from the industry observing that could have granted me auditions or parts. The acting coach became enraged that he hit the wall, dismissed the class, and asked me to stay after class. The last time, I was asked to stay after class was in fourth grade because I rolled a roll of candy to my friend.

I did apologize to my acting coach and in future classes I received critiques in stride. Thereafter, I would have many experiences with receiving critiques from my acting coach and classmates toward my journey to stardom including a critique by Allen Payne, from one of Tyler Perry's shows, House of Paynes who visited this acting class. It was a scene he observed whereas I played a crazy person and I had raised my blouse. He let me know that there is so much in my being—my stage presence that I didn't have to do some of the antics I performed. Wow, indeed! Just thinking about that day, I remember details like it was yesterday including his tone and expressions. I am thankful for Brooklyn McLinn, acting coach for having invited his friend to class. All across-the-board, he has been the best acting coach I have had thus far because of the many inspiring stories that were shared, learning the skill to be able to drop into the emotions of a character immediately, select and present monologues, determine appropriate character analysis, effectively use of stage sets, and to discuss scenes and films for the purpose of learning to become a star. I anticipate the day that I will be able to thank him for being a dynamic and inspirational acting coach during an acceptance speech for an Oscar.

Experience as an Acting Coach

Compelled to stay active in the entertainment industry when I moved back to Nevada, I applied to become an acting coach. Well, I didn't see any auditions whereas I would fit the descriptions and I needed income so that's what led me to apply for my first paid acting coach position. I submitted my acting and teaching resume as well as my teaching credential with the hopes that the employer would grant me the opportunity to become a first time paid acting coach. The only experience I had was from acting as an acting coach for the actors and actresses on my sets of Journey to Stardom Productions. It was three months later that I would gain that position at $35 an hour. Yes, the most hourly rate I've made thus far in the entertainment industry.

It is truly amazing how the dots are connecting on my journey to stardom. In the state of Nevada is where I attended an acting class in preparation for an International Talent Showcase and then to become an acting coach for the same purpose just at a different hotel. Truly Amazing!

Propelling Dreams

Now that I am not shy, have worked as an acting coach, writing scripts for my production company, and ready to audition for any part whereas I fit the descriptions, I'm on course to fulfill my dreams. Nonetheless, my current finances are insufficient to consistently pursue the auditioning process but what I am doing is instrumental to my journey to stardom. Simultaneously, I teach children which incorporates my other childhood dream to become a teacher. Indeed working as an acting coach incorporates teaching, acting, and directing.

It makes me wonder if I would have shared with my first college counselor that I wanted to be a teacher and a star would that have changed my course in life. Unfortunately, I had an unpleasant experience when I went to consult with the high-school counselor in my last year of high-school.

First of all, I had made many attempts to meet with the counselor and I don't know if it was a school budget issue but I really don't think so because I made appointments. When I finally had the opportunity to speak with the counselor she was eating chips, drinking soda, and if I recall precisely it was chili beans in the bowl she was spooning food from. My impression in high-school was that counselors were big shots. Well, my first impression was not good outside of finding out that I wasn't going to have any problem at getting into a college of my choice. Unfortunately, I let that memory foreshadow my meeting with a college guidance counselor. Well, first of all, he didn't smile as I approached him with a smile so I didn't think that was suitable especially after having learned from somewhere in my childhood that it is appropriate to greet people with a smile.

I remember feeling like I didn't trust the counselor's guidance in fact I remember getting upset and it did seem like I settled for liberal arts just to get in a program because he was a challenge to talk to however it turned out good as far as becoming a teacher. So, I would like to encourage you to write down everything you want to do in life and see how you can manage incorporating them all. Most often people know from when they were children what they would like to become and while adults we learn to synthesize our dreams with reality or settle for what is the least challenging.

So wouldn't it be great if childhood dreams, for example, to become a star and a teacher would be cultivated in schools? Specifically, if instead of students being instructed to write their name at the top of a sheet of paper and write their short and long- term goals, what about having students write a list of goals without the arrangement of short versus long term goals? Teachers could incorporate those lists into lessons for the purpose of cultivating informative students about various dreams whether they occur quickly or after a longer period of time. This lesson would inevitably remove the barrier of being shy about sharing personal goals, students would gain information toward their individual goals, and would allow the freedom to dream in the present and keep hope alive vibrantly into adulthood.

In retrospect, I wanted to be a star from childhood but I always envisioned it as when I became an adult because I considered it to be a long-term goal. Neither did I visualize or write down how my life would look as a result of being a star until 2013. The only thing I visualized repeatedly was being on stage and people clapping for me. Share your dreams with other people because you never know who may be able to assist you with your journey and moreover who you will inspire along the way. Consequently, I was inspired by my cousin, Cherise to write a book because she shared her dream with me.

Chapter VII
Observation, Location, and Preparation

The Dynamics of the Monique Show

The Monique Show intrigued me because of the line-up of guests who would night after night inspire me. When it went off the air, I was so sad because I looked forward to learning from the guests. Also, the show came on just before I went to sleep and it propelled me to dream of being on various television and movie sets. Also, I could relate to the effort of losing weight toward improving my television appearance because I've heard that people look approximately ten pounds more than their actual weight. Weight-loss is a challenge.

The spotlight on the effort to lose weight was also inspiring to me because I had been trying to lose weight so many times. I did not focus on the effort during my weight loss attempts just numbers on the scale. For example, I was approaching 190 pounds at that time so instead of eating ice cream while watching the Monique Show I started writing notes and creating lines for my next opportunity to do Stand-Up Comedy toward my effort of weight loss because I began to substitute ice cream for writing and preparation for appearing in front of audiences. Also, the show seemed to be so exciting to Monique that I was motivated to try hosting a show. After sharing many stories about guests of the Monique Show to a musician, he rearranged his studio similar to the likeness of her show. It was a nice surprise and I had fun pretending to be a national talk show host for the first time.

Living in the Entertainment Capital of the World

Just to know so many stars perform in Las Vegas it is exciting to reside in Las Vegas again after the varied experiences I have had in the entertainment industry. In the event that you are reading this book in a different state other than California, Nevada, New York, or Atlanta be encouraged that there are different venues that can be used to practice the craft of acting. For example, libraries, recreation centers, and senior citizen homes are locations outside of the traditional locations used to practice the craft of entertainment.

Specifically, schools, nightclubs, background work, you-tube and other social media sites are examples of traditional locations to practice the craft of acting. I am hoping to build my production company in the near future in Las Vegas, Nevada after considering the fact that there are many people that travel back and forth to California for auditions. Creating demo reels for actors and actresses is my first endeavor at furthering exposure for my production company. I have learned to work with what I have and plan for a well-rounded future. Everyday is a new day to stay to course on a plan as well as prepare for auditions.

Taking Your Desire to be a Star Serious

I have already imagined myself being interviewed by well-known stars at major television studios in Hollywood California about my accomplishments. It is passion and business involved in becoming a star. Acting classes are not free. The auditioning process is filled with passion but it is a business too. For example, aside of the cost of the demo reel and headshots, the portfolio folder/binder that holds your demo reel, resume, and headshots are an expense.

In addition, it is also beneficial to have an elegant pen just in case you need a pen to sign-in. Some people are looking to see how prepared you really are as an evaluation of work ethic. Aside of that, many people accidentally take pens to their seats after signing the sign-in sheet. Another concept to consider is sometimes you are emailed sides for an audition as well as your character sides once you land a part. So ink for your printer or money for printing at a print shop is an expense.

Actors and actresses personal attire, hair, and make-up are all about being about the business. For example, if you dress and look the part of a character at an audition it just may communicate the message that you are that character before you even smile or speak. Also business is in the manner and strength of a handshake because it sends signals about your personality, work ethic, confidence, etc....Overhead expenses such as your rent/mortgage, cell phone, gas/bus fare, car insurance, food, and hygiene are taken into account as your personal business as preparation for your next gig/part. Overall, trying to stay in good health is an expense. Additionally, if you elect to pay for a gym membership it will be an investment toward your health and acting career. During the time I lived between my car and that motel, I used to study my lines while walking on the treadmills because I overheard an actor explain how endorphins---positive emotion sensors in your brain assisted with the memorization process of learning lines. The activity did help me.

In essence, when taking your desire to be a star serious it will behoove you to design a business plan so that you will be better prepared for the journey of preparation prior to auditioning encompassing your living situation and appearance. Furthermore, with a business plan in place it will provide strategic direction and once you begin paying for items that you can use as tax deductions because you are an entrepreneur you want to have an itemization process to keep your receipts in order as well. Indeed, you may even want to purchase a fictitious name since you become a walking business and your own billboard sign in the entertainment business. So, seriously consider those concepts in your business plan too.

Resume Towards Becoming a Star

It was an intimidating time to acquire my first entry for my acting resume. From that International Talent Showcase I attended, I learned of the Backstage Newspaper includes opportunities for auditions. Well, I didn't have the Internet at the time to sign up for access to the newspaper online and my computer was in storage anyway. So, I traveled across town to purchase the newspaper because it is not sold at every convenient store. Then, I was encouraged to use the Internet at my local library to remove the newspaper and gas expense to acquire the newspaper. Then, I learned that there was still an expense to view the newspaper online. Determination and perseverance is imperative for success. I ate less at a fast-food place in order to save money to purchase the newspaper from across town. The goal to learn of an audition from this newspaper paid off and I was casted as part of a theatre ensemble.

Also, in the beginning I felt intimidated by other actresses that seemed to be in the business longer than me or at least seemed more comfortable in the waiting rooms of auditions. Also, when other actresses seemed like it was nothing to the process of acting. However I have learned that it is okay to be the new person on the scene because you are considered a fresh face and there are directors that appreciate the eagerness and novelty of beginning the pursuit of becoming a great actor or actress. So keep trying to do your best and learn all that you can, your efforts will be recognized and pay-off.

If you have already experienced being discouraged by even the closest people to you, it will be okay because some people only believe what they can see. They are called naysayers partially because they do want to see you prosper but they just don't know how much withal you have or may not have seen your perseverance kick tail. Also when you become an actor or actress most often people immediately want to see you doing something but they don't realize how serious the business can be. For example, they don't know about the various skills it takes to put on a scene and the differences between theatre and television and so much more because they have not studied the craft.

Thank goodness for the televised shows like American Idol, as an example because it provides background perspective of the hard work it takes to become a star and how it incorporates the audition process, interview, rehearsals, commercial work, interviews, and constructive criticism at its best. Based on that information more people are able to see the mantra of the business to become a star versus simply watching a television show or listening to songs on their car radio. It takes so much to build a resume.

Likewise if you are a triple threat in the manner that you can sing, dance, and act keep them present. For example, based on information I have learned, if I had all of those talents I would audition for all three at various times so that I could quickly gain entries under each talent. That way when I auditioned, the decision makers in the auditioning room would know that I was a triple threat based on my resume and I wouldn't have to tell them, they would just ask me to validate the notion that I am a triple threat.

I was told to build my theatre experience first and then pursue other genres of the entertainment industry. Certainly, I should have taken that information as a suggestion and not literally especially after believing I was a commercial actor. Additionally, I love to laugh and I was a salesperson aside of being a teacher which in all actuality teaching is a quality of salesmanship so I was unaware at the time why I didn't pursue

Stand-Up Comedy. After reflecting about my novice career thus far, I did not have a plan and although I was runner-up in the Stand-Up comedy division in Miami, I was just operating and easily persuaded about how to approach my acting career. Strategic planning and stern focus will assist with becoming a star.

In essence, I started out the gate with the auditioning process after leaving Miami to build my acting resume without a business plan, financial plan, a projection map encompassing my future living quarters, weight maintenance, or about having an acting coach to continually practice the craft and consult with when sides were provided. So, attending workshops and classes is where an aspiring actor/actress can begin. Participating in local community plays at libraries, recreational centers, and churches are instruments for smart, broke, and want to be stars to practice the craft of acting without paying for acting classes.

Similarly participating in an International Talent Showcases is an ideal vehicle to utilize for the purpose of being seen by many decision makers in the entertainment industry from various genres and divisions. International Talent Showcases are usually held over the course of a couple of days in various states. You can investigate some A-list stars are a result of participating in International Talent Showcases. Also, many writers, directors, and producers look for new talent there. It's just really nice when you can audition for as many of them as possible at one time.

Audition Search Engines

There is another avenue to audition for many decision makers in the industry and that is by using free social medias or by paying for various search engines that permit you to upload your resume, headshots, and demo reels. When casting agents need to look for talent some prefer to begin with what is available at their fingertips—technology. Thereafter, you would be called for in-person audition. Nevertheless the more vehicles you can use to market your skills the more likely you will be noticed. Moreover, the more prepared you are to share your talent(s) at optimum level the better propensity you have to be casted for the job.

Chapter VIII
Happenstance

Influential Circle

The following passages are for the purpose of demonstrating how important it is to surround your-self with elevating people:

There was a time I had to pick up my aunt and uncle and help them move with my compact car. At that time I was living in a hotel and was using that cane my grandmother let me use following that hip injury from being on set in the woods. I wanted to help them feel better about their ill circumstances so I took them to the 24hr restaurant I used to sit for long periods of time when I couldn't afford the motel fee. It is fun talking to them and I spent a great deal of time helping them the best way I could aside of moving them in with me and increasing my hotel rate during that timeframe in their life.

No disrespect intended toward my aunt and uncle. I just want to provide the facts that there is a need to help those that you can that are less fortunate than you but there is a need to be in company of people that can elevate your thinking and challenge you to grant yourself permission to dream and acquire thousands of dollars as a star.

Might of fact this particular aunt can really sing and she was the one that was with me when I went to an office building for the purpose of leasing office space for my various businesses as a salesperson. At that time I was trying to build businesses that I could use to sustain me financially while I pursued a massive amount of auditions because I was going to take a semester off from teaching to pursue my dream. Also, I was finally living in an apartment after two years of living in motels, my car, and a hotel. Unfortunately, the lease amount was too much. The gentleman that showed me the office space asked what my intentions were for the office space. My need to share information propelled me to give details of the items I would be selling and the days and times I would like to open and close. In addition, I shared details about my pursuit of becoming a star and

about the Worldwide Star Search event
that was approaching. He would later pay my car
payment and give me money to by clothes that
assisted with getting to the event, dressed
appropriately, and with winning first place.

After we were shown the office space, the
gentleman invited us to his music studio after
questioning whether or not we could sing. When he
learned that my aunt could sing he invited us
inside his music studio where he had come from to
see what business we were there for inside
another office. He didn't hear us talking loud or
anything, he had a camera system and that's how
he was able to see us. My aunt sang for him and his
band. They wanted her to come back and sing on
some tracks but she knew my uncle would be
jealous from her being around other men in that
atmosphere. I tried to encourage her to sing on
those tracks with the hopes that could be their
ticket out of motels especially since she wasn't
going to have to pay any studio time. People that
really don't see entertainment as a real business
walk away from opportunities such as the above
example. Although, I wasn't shy about singing
outside of my house by this time, I just knew I
needed to know many words to a song and I
honestly still needed singing lessons to learn how
to control my voice and many more skills of the art
of singing. I practically begged her to let me pick
her up that weekend to capitalize on the

opportunity. To no avail she has not been to his studio since then.

Nevertheless, helping and spending time with my aunt and uncle helped lead me to meeting that gentleman at his music studio who would later provide me the forum to pretend to be a talk show host for upcoming artist as well as the producer of my first track created by people I auditioned for my company, Journey to Stardom Productions. So thus far, I have a soundtrack in production for my company, a couple of episodes completed, many more episodes in the editing process, and my first book with the help of this gentleman, family, and friends.

In essence, even though you may not be in the company of millionaires or prominent decision makers in the entertainment industry on a daily basis just like me, please note people that may be naysayers or not even have a roof over their heads can help you. You may not realize it while you're doing your best to help them through the valleys of their life experiences but in time seeds will sprout into something beautiful or becomes weeds that will need to be plucked. I encourage you to be as nice and respectful as possible at all times so that you won't regret anything.

Relationship

After learning that leasing an office space was out of my budget, I had to retreat to another plan, yet I had not written a back-up plan. While I admired how beautiful my aunt can sing, I did

notice he was observing me and I thought
he was really handsome but I wasn't expecting a
guy of such fineness would be interested in me
anyway so I took the observation as a grain of salt
although I was weighing 145 pounds, weave was
whipped, and I was dressed nice from teaching my
class that day. When my aunt finished singing a
song as his band played, we listened to all of the
wonderful compliments she received and the
request granted for her to sing on some tracks, I
was ready to leave especially since I had to drop
her off across town from my apartment and had to
go to work that following morning.

Before we left a gentleman asked if we could
exchange numbers after running his fingers across
mines. At that time, I had snapped at him about
touching my hand. It was a slight sign that I had
embarrassed him in front of his band. I would later
find out he was hammered after I left. To this day
his band calls me schoolteacher. We have been in a
relationship off and on for approximately ten years
but always maintained being friends.

So the above information is a testimony that
when you are doing business, people take notes.
Likewise, although I initially tried to help myself, in
midstream at the same location I began to help my
aunt who could inadvertently help my uncle
financially if the tracks would have been made and
sold. As a result, meeting this producer turned out
to be an unwritten business plan because he has
helped me financially for many years and I haven't

sold any kind of weight-loss, make-up, or insurance since meeting him.

In addition, when he let me use his music studio as a location to audition people for skits and toward a collaborative soundtrack for my company, many songs were created and incomplete. During the process of writing this book he has worked to complete unfinished songs so that my first soundtrack for Journey to Stardom Productions will be ready for me to overlay music on scenes that I have filmed.

It is exciting to have another project waiting for me and at the same time it is a challenge because I want to do so well with each project. Nonetheless, you just don't know what will kick off your major success at times. So since I'm not a traditional triple threat, I am motivated to capitalize on what I have that can help me to achieve stardom and you can too.

Remember sharing your dreams and aspirations with people can undeniably help you. Don't be shy. Speak up and let the world know you are a star too!

Chapter IX

Star Encounters

Radio Experience

The opportunity to work at the American Radio Network as a disc jockey was fun because I was able to use a microphone. I was only able to do that for a couple of months because I didn't have the money to pay even the small fee for the air and booth time. However during that time I met a nice radio coach who introduced me to Rahm Lee and I was able to interview him on my station. That was a highlight outside of that radio coach inviting various talents to my school for career day such as Nipsey Russel.

Hill Harper, was the guy sitting on a couch in the lounge nearest the door on my first day at American Radio Network as a disc jockey. It was the upcoming extraordinary, Hill Harper! I loved the respect that was given to him. What was said was that he didn't care to have small talk with people because he was always studying. He did have a book in his hand, a notebook on his lap and a backpack next to him so I believed everything that was said about him and I wasn't one of those women who began talking after the radio coach left the room. The other women demonstrated a lack of respect toward the tone the radio coach tried to implement before he left out of the lounge. Hill Harper left out of the room shortly afterwards possibly due to the abrupt chatter.

More Encounters with Stars at Steve Harvey's 10th Annual Hoodie Awards

It was not long after I relocated to Las Vegas, Nevada that I found a job on the Internet for the Steve Harvey's 10th Annual Hoodie Awards. The job was through an agency that he uses when he does events in Las Vegas, Nevada. Someday, I will like to work with Steve Harvey's staff again. The great amount of people that I came in contact with was a dream team. He has a great team of people working with him! My job was to wave a large purple finger for the purpose of directing patrons to different venues at the Mandalay Bay Hotel, MGM Grand Hotel, and at the McCarren Airport. The event took place on my birthday weekend. It was an extraordinary gift. It did not feel like work because it was so much fun.

When I was at the airport. I was there waving a large purple finger that many people wanted to buy as a souvenir when Dr. Steve Perry and his wife entered the baggage area. I knew I saw him before but I simply did my job with reassuring them that they were in the right area and that I was going to direct them to the sign-in area and from there they would be escorted to a car to be driven to a hotel. Educators are stars in my book too.

In addition, there was this frenzy about Tyler Perry would be coming to the baggage area in the near future. Time and more time passed but I really believe the person I said was Tyler Perry, I believe was correct because no other tall man of his

stature with sunglasses entered the
baggage area thereafter.

Tasha Smith and her husband came down the
escalator nearest me and I knew it was Tasha
Smith even though she had on sunglasses too. Just
think, I attended her acting class but she was not
there because she just recently began working on a
set at Tyler Perry's Studio in Atlanta. Greetings
were exchanged and again I provided the same
information as I did to Dr. Steve Perry and his wife.
A person on the other side of Tasha Smith and her
husband said she would be escorting them to their
car. My response was okay, but I had you covered I
was going to take good care of you all. Tasha Smith
replied, "Thank You." In hindsight, I do remember
hearing her sharing words of encouragement over
the acting coach's cell phone during acting class.
The acting class in Santa Monica, California was
originally her class. It was during the time she was
beginning to work on a show with Michael Jai
White who I did see as well who walked really fast
past a group of purple fingers.

Terrence J and a woman with a dog came down
the escalator. The luggage looked extremely heavy
so I offered to give him a break with something at
least unto the sign-in sheet area. He declined the
assistance. He had to wait for his assistant to exit
the elevator with more pieces of luggage. So, I was
able to make a little small talk with them and
admire the cute little dog.

At the MGM Hotel, I got a chance to listen and laugh to what Cheryl Underwood was saying to a group of people that were at a sign-in area while I waited alongside some other purple finger wavers for a van to take us to another hotel. I was told that I did such a good job with making the patrons happy and well informed that someone told someone else to have me work with the concierge office to further assist guests of the Steve Harvey's Hoodie Awards.

At the Mandalay Bay Hotel I had the opportunity to assist Lenny Williams in a computer area for the purpose of retrieving his airplane tickets. That was so special. It was just like spending time with my grandfather, Daddy Gene.

Stephanie Mills was standing and waiting for someone not far from the concierge office, so we exchanged greetings. One of Steve Harvey's employees knows Keith Sweat so when he came into the lobby they greeted one another and she introduced me to him and he greeted me with a handshake. Wow!

An assistant of Anthony Hamilton was waiting for him to enter the lobby. She was going to meet with him and escort him to his car that would take him to the airport. I asked her how she became his assistant. She explained that she was looking for a job as an assistant and he happened to be the person offering the job opportunity. Eventually, she thought too much time had transpired so two of Steve Harvey's employees, Anthony Hamilton's assistant, and myself took the elevator to the penthouse room where he was still packing. He was hilarious to assist. It was extremely fun. Of course that was my first time thus far being in a penthouse and it had a luxurious view! I helped by carrying a gift basket to the concierge's office. While on the elevator he thanked me and asked me my name. Aw.... Once he appeared in the lobby, many people asked to take pictures with him. His assistant asked if I wanted to take a picture with him. Of course, I denied the offer at first because I was trying to be professional and not take advantage of the special opportunity granted to me from maintaining professionalism over the past couple of days. She insisted because she thought it was only fair because I just helped him with a heavy gift basket and he really wasn't going to mind. So, I went ahead and obliged the offer and I took into consideration that it was the last day of the event too. Indeed he was very nice about taking the picture with me and it was his assistant who took the picture using my cell phone. Aw!

Additionally, there were many people whereas we kept running into one another throughout Steve Harvey's 10th Annual Hoodie Awards event that I hope will get a chance to read this book and to learn that they made me feel like a star too. In addition there were many couples and I would compliment them on their change of clothes or just small talk because they were having so much fun with being involved with the event that although I don't know their names, you're stars in my book too. Furthermore, I am extremely thankful to Steve Harvey and his staff for a magnificent venue and well-organized event that allowed me to experience: encounters of very nice patrons and stars. I still have a purple finger and yellow t-shirt from this event as souvenirs.

Chapter X

Constructive Time

What Do I Do in the Meantime?

The meantime is a critical time during a journey to stardom. For instance, I've learned to be proactive about my acting career. It is imperative to find things that will improve your talents or the skills you want to enhance. Attending workshops, classes, watching movies, studying your favorite actors, reading more books about the craft, and videotaping yourself rehearsing various character lines are a handful of things that can be done along the way to stardom.

Similarly, the subheading above is what prompted me to physically begin writing this book versus wallowing in the inspired stage. For example as you read this book it will be an example of how I spent my time while on my journey to stardom. Also, this book will be a testimony that in the meantime of being broke and wanting to inspire people to continue to press forward even when going through a valley of their life there is something that can be done.

In addition, setting a detailed schedule in preparation for stardom has helped me thus far. For example, I made appointments with family and friends to create a schedule of communication that permitted me to write half of this book in approximately three weeks. Also, I created a schedule for exercising and designed a menu that would not take much time away from writing.

Literally, I was on schedule for a tutoring school and once a month as an acting coach but I devised a work schedule for my journey to stardom as well. Precisely, I worked three hours before and after my tutoring schedule so I matched the six hours I worked for someone else to work on Journey to Stardom Productions. On days off from the employer's job I worked as many hours as I wanted. Knowing how you operate will benefit you, for instance, I was afraid to give myself permission to take a break to organize some papers because I knew I would get off task so I put the papers in a bag to stay until I finished this book.

Reinventing yourself is a phrase that I forgot about because I let myself get consumed with my current financial status. Maybe writing a book as a novice actress as a way of giving back will be viewed as being something on a small scale to many people but it will always be an endearing effort toward helping people in my time of need because it was something I could do at that time in my life to regain momentum on my journey to stardom.

Also, the state of worry about obtaining a day job in education that will afford me the financial freedom to buy my own food again has been perplexing. Indeed grateful for having an EBT card, job—just over broke, and family/friend's support but I want more. For example, at the time of writing this section of the book, my car had one-eighth of a tank of gas, just about $4 in my bank account, a dollar bill and about $2 in change in my purse but I still had the passion to make a difference even through my adversity.

I wore spanks while typing since I wasn't exercising as much as I was before writing this book. I listened to music and typed during commercials of television shows. Also, I talked to family and friends on scheduled days to update them on my progress. I listened to people that could jog my memory by asking me questions about my novice experience in the entertainment industry. I took naps. I read and skimmed books. Most of the time I ate bowls of frozen vegetables, dry cereal, drank a cup of coffee a day, lemon water, plain water, and oatmeal for the real meal because I had already maxed my EBT-food card in the effort of buying healthy foods that cost more.

Ultimately, in the meantime of stardom, there is time to strategize and work toward building your brand.

CHAPTER XI

Real Talk

Why did I write this book?

Foremost, I wrote this book to share my experiences and give insight to people who think about pursuing acting as a career. In addition, I wanted to make money so that I could finish my doctorate degree.

Likewise it would be a testimony of how there are people who do want to pursue an acting career but without enough money and bare necessities make it a challenge to manifest their desire to pursue their dreams expediently. This book would allow me to motivate people to pursue their dreams and recognize that they may have to take another avenue to get to stardom. For example, I would have never thought in a million years that in approximately six months after earning a master's degree that I would be: homeless, gained an agent, in need of headshots, and gas money to get to auditions. Fortunately, through perseverance and determination, I made it to newspapers and national television.

Years passed and I always felt a need to talk to many people about my journey to stardom in the hopes that it would motivate others that are smart, broke, and want to be a star that things can be done while treading through the valleys of their journey to stardom as well and inform them that it will ultimately help them build characters.

Similarly, once I realized that I was building character through lack of finances that would inevitably help me in the future as an actress, I began to become a motivator.

My energy changed to focus on the possibility that I could propel my star quality into reality whereas it would shine brightly. I realized there were things I could do even while I was broke toward making my star shine. I began exercising in the effort of looking my best for when I do begin the auditioning process and Stand-Up Comedy again as examples. In addition, I began to write comedy material, scripts for shows I plan to direct and produce or just sell. The focalized worried energies began to gain a positive momentum. My effort began to spearhead the building of my brand in the manner of a variety of other aspects amongst the entertainment industry alongside acting, writing, directing, and producing. Those ideals will be written in another book.

Another reason, I wanted to write this book was because during my auditioning valleys, I yearned for an avenue to discuss at length with someone that understood the journey without having to answer why do I want to pursue a career in entertainment when it's a gamble on success and when I have so much education behind me. I believe that other people with advanced degrees that have been homeless and are homeless is because it's more than a notion that a heightened passion for another career has been repressed due to fear and shyness; thereby encumbering their longevity on that job/career. So, I wanted a forum to share with many people for generations to come to remember that most often millionaires and billionaires didn't gain their success by being fearful of doing what they loved or shyly built their businesses, so their acting career should begin as a business and thrive as a business. Also to remember intelligence and passion impels success. In contrast, intelligence coupled with fear stifles epic success as well as passion and self-confidence.

In addition, because I learned to understand the mantra of having a back-up plan with education and a career in order to sustain financially if my dreams didn't emerge; yet I still experienced being financially constrained without thoroughly pursuing my ultimate career dream. I wanted to share that there are pockets in current lifestyles of people that aspire to be a star where they can still prepare to become a star.

Additionally, I wanted to use this book as a platform to help provide encouragement for aspiring actors to cease from being considerate toward feelings of pessimistic people in their lives especially their loved ones. Indeed, I heard a lot of pessimism from people that weren't even in the business and it is preposterous to allow people to spoil your dreams based on hearsay. It took me decades to learn that.

Also, from learning about the concept, back-up plan in elementary school became the only plan and as much as I do enjoy teaching, I still want more and that is to be a star. It would have been nice to be told as well to pursue my most favored dream along the way and have faith that it will prevail.

Additionally, I wanted to share that I understood how it feels to be stereotyped and wanting so much to prove there is more to you than others' perspective of you. Acting provides that vehicle to rupture stereotypes and Stand-Up Comedy allows you to vent. Certainly, all of the roles played by actors and actresses are not based on their personal experiences it's just that they have learned to channel energies from other events whether personal or from learned studies of other people to drive those roles.

For example, Stand-Up Comedy is a forum for me to vent and I had to learn that people that have known me since I was a child don't get it when I'm not speaking politically correct and cracking jokes especially when their jokes used to be about me. If you want to be a star and have been pursuing the journey you can attest to how some people do not accept your thirst for stardom. Unfortunately, they may have become so complacent in their lives and possibly forgot how to dream because of so much turmoil that they have experienced, they purposefully or inadvertently encumber your dreams.

On the other hand, there are people who just don't look beyond the trees to see the mountains.

For example, this guy began to call me, Ms. Hollywood. In the beginning it sounded complimentary but I later learned it was sarcasm because the common thread thereafter was about me looking for a job that matched his work hours.

Most people have heard of that cliché, sometimes you have to get yourself out of the way to make progress. Indeed that is a fact just like it took me two years to get back to writing a book. At times, in order to get things done you have to give yourself permission to stop communicating with naysayers, or re-examine how you are spending your time. It is harder to travel uphill with extra weight on your back literally and physically.

Ultimately, the reason why I wrote this book was not only due to being low on funds that prevented me from enrolling in my next doctorate degree class, but because of the fact that my birthday was approaching as well. I was indeed emotional about not completing my doctorate degree by that time so I felt like I had to fulfill a void. Writing a book happened to be one of the goals on my list that I could do for free to help people that want to be stars just like me. Likewise, even if I didn't have a computer, I had pen, paper, and access to a local library to write a book that I could use with the hope, it would be a hook to get Tyler Perry to take a look and help me on my journey to stardom.

Chapter XII

Questions and Answers

Question: Am I a triple threat?

Answer: Yes, maybe not in the dominant standpoint of singing, dancing, and acting. Enjoyably, I am a triple threat by means of acting, directing, and coaching. They all encompass teaching. Based on what I've learned as well, it matters a great deal to do what you enjoy and when work becomes play that is the best work.

Question: Who is your celebrity crush?

Answer: Tyreese aka Black-Tie. Why? Not only because he was the first star that is in my age group that I had the opportunity to meet and have a conversation with but I respected his honesty and sincerity. Outside of him being such a handsome, talented, and debonair guy, he also seems to have maintained his loving and thoughtful spirit encompassing the gift of holding conversations of substance for the purpose of inspiring people to be at their best.

I met Tyreese when I went to a club to see Shaquille O'Neal perform his song, Outstanding. Tyreese was sitting in a semi-secluded area at first but as so many women kept approaching him I guess he decided he could manage the amount of women in a more orderly fashion if he sat in a booth. The booth was technically a four-person booth but six women was able to fit at a time. The side I sat on was on the same side as Tyreese but some skinny lady rushed to get in front of me. Of course, I put on my nice as pie attitude and let that roll off of my shoulder although I really wanted to be shoulder to shoulder with Tyreese.

At any rate the same manner in which the footage of Tyreese and La-La having a conversation about her wedding on a reality show La-La had or a reality show where Tyreese and Brandi met and conversed over food is the same manner in which Tyreese conducted himself years ago during the time I sat at the table with him. The topic of conversation at the table with Tyreese was about appearances. I was like oh, oh here we go and I'm sitting on one cheek at the end of the booth on the other side of a petite lady while leaning around her head to see him with my fat pressed against the table. He started providing observations of our appearance and began with the first lady sitting across from him and then around to the lady who sat directly next to him. While I waited my turn I remember holding in my stomach as much as I could and even trying to squeeze the fat on my shoulders in before he got to me. When it was my turn he told me that I had a pretty face, nice teeth, beautiful smile, and I just needed to lose some weight. I look forward to meeting him considering the fact that I have lost weight and even had a tummy tuck.

Question: Did you participate in school plays?

Answer: Yes, I participated in as many plays as possible especially after learning from the Rodger

Thomas acting class that it didn't pay to be shy if I wanted to be an actress. Just a note, when I became a teacher I began writing school plays that were performed during school assemblies.

Question: How do you feel about wanting to be a star since elementary school and almost at the point of completing a doctorate degree?

Answer: I certainly understand speculation that I may have given up on my dream of becoming a star after the long period of time. However in all actuality I have been working toward stardom in intervals. Now, I'm ready to get back in the game like a number one racehorse going all the way to legacy status!

Question: What was your oddest memory you reflected on when studying for an acting class?

Answer: The oddest memory was definitely the memory about babysitting that cat for my brother and his girlfriend in lieu of sleeping in my car. I had to study a character and provide as many specific details as possible. In order to be creative I chose to write about that cat. Just to be specific about why I chose to write a reflection about that cat is because it seemed like it talked and had personality. For example, I called the cat's name so that it would be inside while I went to work. Well, I didn't see the cat so I closed the door and finished getting ready for work. Shortly afterwards, I heard knocking on the screen-door. It was that cat. It actually sounded like it was fussing at me—like you called me and then I can't get in. It walked in and looked me up and down. Then it walked past me and turned around and sounded like it said something else. I hurried up and left to go to work.

Question: Where will you be in five years on your journey to stardom?

Answer: I will be in California acting on a television sitcom, receiving revenues from writing varied genres, conducting motivational speeches, Stand-Up Comedy, more television shows and from being an acting coach to support the financial position to provide for my family encompassing vacations. Additionally, I will be physically fit and would have had a little liposuction on my waist. I will be driving a silver Mercedez Benz. Paid off a mortgage and other bills that would have cleaned up my credit report and completed my doctorate degree in instructional leadership to assist with being an acting coach which is also considered an instructional leader.

Question: What has been your favorite audition so far?

Answer: One of the auditions for a Crash the Superbowl commercial I applied for was retrieved from an audition talent search engine. The director, a very tall man from the audition room, to the rest of the characters and staff made the experience so much fun because everyone worked together, laughed, smiled, and was overwhelmingly considerate. When I walked into the audition room, the director had a cool disposition and a nice hat on. The room was set up like an airport and I auditioned to be casted as a security guard. The atmosphere was detailed—set up like a real set versus other auditions that use a table, camera, and unfavorable demeanors. The director instructed the tall guy and my self to really give another guy a hard time about trying to get a bag of potato chips on the airplane. We worked that guy over to the point all three of us were casted in that commercial. Awesome!

Also from that audition experience, I learned that character study or from building rapport in a waiting room can produce awesome results including future jobs with the same cast like in the world of theatre.

Question: Have you met a star inadvertently?

Answer: Yes, I met Steve Russell from the R&B group, Troop. I was at another music studio auditioning rappers/actors on a green screen for my production company, Journey to Stardom Productions. Initially I hoped to meet him considering the fact his gold records were displayed so exquisitely. Unknowingly, one day, Steve Russell was in the studio booth. When he opened the door, I looked and I was like, great I finally get to meet you. He laughed. I was formally introduced to him. He was a gentleman. I conversed with him at the studio on another day while we all ate lunch.

Also, I met Katt Williams after a friend asked me to go see one of his comedy shows in Vegas,

November 9, 2013. I asked Katt Williams would it be okay to add him into my book, he replied, "yes, did you meet me in person and it's true, right?" I replied, yes. I didn't have a cell phone that allowed picture taking so, I missed that opportunity but a friend of mine took the picture.

Question: Do you have any family members that are in the entertainment industry?

Answer: I do not have any blood relatives in the industry but I do have a married in cousin that is a star. My blood first cousin's father is a brother to Yo-Yo's father. I remember going to a party with my cousin who she and   Yo-Yo are first cousins and I was pregnant at the time. Undoubtedly, I looked like I was going to burst. I went on the dance floor anyway. After all, dancing is a form of exercise. When Yo-Yo came over to the floor after talking with some people, I didn't ask her for an autograph. Instead, I asked her to rub her stardom on my huge stomach. The daughter that I was pregnant with at that time can sing, rap, and freestyle too.

Question: Are any of the characters in your script, you?

Answer: Many portions of the characters personalities are indeed mine. I laughed and cried during the time I wrote the script because I wrote from realities of my heart and about the people that helped to inspire me to pursue my dream. Also, I could see the script being played out by members of my family, friends, and superstars.

Ultimately, I have envisioned this play on screen someday.

Question: What do you think about the historical collaboration between Tyler Perry and Oprah Winfrey?

Answer: I think it is the greatest duo ever in the acting/television realm of entertainment. I'm not married now but I dream of a day that I meet a man that is just as supportive as Tyler Perry is for Oprah Winfrey. In addition, he has inspired my creativity so much that I screamingly dream to be in front of the camera acting crazy just like, Madea. He is the most instrumental person that has inspired me to write my first script in line to be published.

Likewise, I would love to become a talk show host for novice college students and have distinguished educators and their spouses to mentor them on the show such as, Dr. Steve Perry and his wife. The serious part of my brain is driven like Oprah Winfrey and Tyler Perry's example of propelling information, tilling emotions, and education through books and film.

--I await the day that I will be able to act on screen as wild as Tyler Perry's Madea and motivate students like Oprah Winfrey on OWN.

Question: Is this book an audition for Tyler Perry?

Answer: This would be a serious audition. In all actuality, I can see it perceived in that manner. With that said, this book will indeed provide extensive background that can be developed into roles I could play. The concept of a book being an audition is interesting. Auditions are usually quick but this book will be recurrent.

Question: What is your favorite movie outside of Tyler Perry because I know you love all of Tyler Perry's work?

Answer: Okay, I'll speak on another favorite movie: Tom Hanks, The Terminal. I watched this movie at least thirty times. Initially, I watched the movie over to my brother and his girlfriend's apartment during that time I babysat their cat while they went on vacation. The movie made me cry so much but I watched it over and over that week because I didn't connect to any of the other movies they had in their collection.

I remember being on set of the show where I wore the police uniform. That television studio has a video store and I asked the cashier if there were any movies by Tom Hank in there, specifically, The Terminal. The cashier looked passed me and I heard a sound that denotes shock and then the cashier turned around to check the system. So what is so special about this movie the cashier had questioned. I told him that it was a heartfelt story about a person not having a home to go to and that it was my present story. Then there was a gasp behind me. I turned around and the group of people that were obviously eavesdropping started talking like they had already been talking. I left out of the store wondering who were those people and why didn't that video store have, The Terminal movie? I still wonder if those people were connected to the staff of that show I was doing background work because that has been the most continuous background work, I've done to date— approximately three weeks.

Later that day, I went to check the movie bin at a 24 hour store and found it for an affordable price. It was like therapy to me so later when I met a co-worker who was going through a similar plight, I let her family have my copy, of The Terminal and they loved it too.

Question: Did you think of the possibility that people may think the word broke in the title may allude to being broke emotionally.

Answer: No. I thought, I was going to have pictures on the front cover that would exemplify the words in the title. However in considering what I have been through in my life the word broke in the facet of emotionally broken, works too. So I didn't add those pictures. Maybe in the future, I will write another book about my experience of being emotionally broken. Thank you.

Question: What is your definition of being financially broke?

Answer: Financially broke is experiencing inefficient income that impedes the allowance of purchases for monthly bare necessities, bills, education, savings, and investments.

CHAPTER XIII

Research Connections

In Tyler Perry's, Don't Make a Black Woman Take Off Her Earrings (2006) he shared, "I hope there is something that...has inspired you and even awakened something in your spirit to motivate you to become an even better human being." Likewise, I hope the sharing of my experiences inspires you to experience your journey to stardom enthusiastically.

When I was overwhelmed with wondering about what other people thought about my dream of becoming a star, I didn't pursue my dream fervently. When I accepted everyone I have known or will encounter is not sold on stardom; I freed myself from being easily discouraged by people who did not share my dream. In so doing, I began to create storyboards, writing speeches, poems, monologues, and material for stand-up comedy as an outlet to dream.

John C. Maxwell wrote, "I will prioritize my life and give focus and energy to those things that give the highest return...Time is the most valuable coin in your life...Your greatest possession is the twenty-four hours you have directly ahead of you...." (2004). Indeed, once I resolved to the fact that I wanted without a shadow of a doubt to become an actress and help people via media, I began scheduling my time for prayer, meals, phone conversations, reading, writing, researching, dreaming, emailing updates to my support team as an accountability system, and time for exercise. Additionally, I rearranged my residence to accommodate a more conducive environment for writing unswervingly.

In addition, John C. Maxwell stated, "[a]n investment in a person ultimately pays the highest return because it can result in changed lives...What life experiences have you had that can help another person?...May thinking become your greatest tool for creating the world you desire" (2003). Likewise, the reason why I wanted to become a teacher was to replicate how I felt when I learned something new as early as elementary school. It was an enlightening experience time after time. Also, I viewed, teachers as stars because they used their attention getting skills to share information they had. So, after brainstorming ideas that I could do to help people that want to become stars became sharing my experiences in a book about information that I know firsthand.

In the interim of writing this book, I read Earvin Johnson's, 32 Ways to Be a Champion in Business: "Create a guiding vision of where you want to go and what you want to do with your life" (2008) and I synthesized how I could implement my thinking into creating a script that would share my desires. Simultaneously it would be a representation of my visions as a teleplay—a story prepared for television production.

"Anchoring is a way to give an experience permanence. We can change our internal representations or our physiology in a moment and create new results, and those changes require conscious thought" (Robbins, 1986). Every time I think of being smart, broke, and wanting to be a star it has encouraged me to take action.

However, it wasn't until I wrote Smart, Broke, and Want to be a Star on paper that I began to build a strategic momentum toward my journey to stardom in lieu of simply allowing those current conditions to overwhelm me. Hopefully when other people read the words: smart, broke, and want to be a star it will be an anchor for motivating progress toward their journey to stardom.

Similarly, when I thought of my finances I would think of what if I earned a degree in the entertainment field instead of the education field, it was an anchor that reminded me of my desire of "finding employment in a creative field is definitely possible with a little ingenuity and a lot of passion" (Levit, 2008). Although, I knew I was capable of acting out roles; I did not think I had enough education or experience to acquire employment as an actress on an episodic television show or a talk show. Subsequently, my thirst for knowledge deterred my passion at that time.

Later, I wondered how I could share with people my congruent plight of gaining education and experience in acting while working in the education field and attending doctoral classes.

Simultaneously, I wondered about a financial outlet that would assist with sharing my experiences and receive income to complete the doctoral program. It would be years ahead that I would read, Prepare to be a Millionaire (Spinks, et al, 2008) about how I could use the Internet to share my experiences to inform people of an authentic account of a smart, broke, and want to be a star enthusiast. Correspondingly, "[w]hat are the different ways people can sell information on the Internet? (Spinks, 2008). That was the precise information that I wanted. "You can package information as e-books, membership sites, templates or tools, courses, or anything. Just be creative." (Spinks, 2008). The information offered in this book was instrumental to imparting credence to being successful via Internet because I didn't have capital to pay for business assistance from a publishing company.

Respectively, reared and raised in middle class South Central-Los Angeles as well as Compton, California, I was aware of the need to earn at least decent money but after becoming an adult I didn't know how to effectively manage money even with a master's degree in education. So, I began to read books regarding wealth. The quote by Allen & Hansen "[s]elf-doubt drowns your dreams. Hesitation holds you hostage. Skepticism scares away your success. You wonder, 'What will they think?' I don't have a degree or a diploma...[there] is a list of billionaires and multimillionaires who

never graduated from college" (2002) was
the premise that led me to believe that if I earned a
college degree or two or go for the gusto and get a
PhD that I would become financially set.

Well, it wasn't until I was a third away from
completion of earning a doctorate degree that I
realized I nourished self-doubt, hesitation,
skepticism, and being a worrywart impeded
seeking the tools needed to successfully earn,
invest, manage, and create passive revenue.
Certainly with a master's degree I could earn a
decent living but based on who's standard and in
what economy? If I wanted to successfully earn
money I wouldn't feel stressed in the occupation
that I was earning money.

In hindsight, I realized I would have gained a
degree in entertainment to prepare for successfully
earning, investing, managing, and creating passive
money. Imagine being a comedian who has a
degree in any area of entertainment chosen and
most often if not all would encourage management
representation. A manager as a comedian could
learn more about money management. Likewise,
footage of say the comedian appearing in a movie
or sitcom that goes into syndication becomes
passive income. Thereby, I hope readers will
congruently and passionately pursue their dreams
and manage their dreams as a business.
Correspondingly as in, Make the Impossible
Possible states "the people you need to meet in
your life are out there, waiting... I'm convinced that

you'll catch the ear of the right crowd and point yourself in the direction of extraordinary experience and meaningful success" (2007).

I don't know if Oprah Winfrey dreamed of being a billionaire when she was a child but I do agree that "[b]etween the movies she produces, books or products she has recommended, her television show, Website, and magazine, her reach is positively tentacular, touching so many people about so many things in so many different ways over...[the] years" (Nelson, 2005). It will be a dream come true when I gain an astronomical audience to inspire.

In Maxwell's, (2002) Running with the Giants it shares, "Noah's Prayer for Us, Dear Lord, Please help my fellow runners to understand the power of one. Speak to them about the unique task You call them... to follow through so that they, too, can make a difference. Amen." Faith, perseverance, and determination has propelled me to write this book and I believe that people will share with me their journey to stardom at http://www.stardom-gate.com because together we can band as one force to help strengthen the need for self-improvement in current and future generations. In view of that, "Oprah Winfrey is the fifth-generation entrepreneur in her family" (Gates II, 2007).

Similarly, you may be head of your household causing you to model self-improvement; therefore having access to the above website could be viewed as a free interactive sounding board—support system. Parallel to the above ideal, Linkner in Disciplined Dreaming states "[o]ne idea is all it takes to change your career...company...region...country...the world...tap into your own brilliant creativity. That one idea is inside you right now. Now it's your turn to let your best creative ideas come out to play" (2011). Oprah Winfrey has set a phenomenal example that one woman can make changes. Likewise, "...from a financial standpoint as it relates to stand-up comedy and movies and produced and then wrote and then cast other [people]...and brought them all together. [Eddie Murphy is that o]ne man [who] did that" (Littleton, 2006). The above information intrigued me to learn about the ability to gain a large audience like Oprah Winfrey and to captivate an audience like Eddie Murphy has, so I learned the phrase "elusive quality—the plus factor..." (Henry & Rogers, 2008). In their book, How To Be A Working Actor it also stated, "[c]ombined life experience, the powers of observation, a love of the work, persistence, and...when they are mesmerized by your performance and the critics finally acknowledge that you have arrived...then all the sacrifices and the hard work will be worth it" (Henry & Rogers, 2008). After reviewing the above characteristics, I assessed my star quality and I await the day that "critics finally acknowledge that [I]...have arrived" too. (Henry & Rogers, 2008).

Smart, broke, and want to be stars: How are we going to ascertain immense attention of critics that can propel acting careers? Farrah Gray specified, "[h]ustle is focusing your dreams into fruition. Hustle is staying with it after everyone else has given up. Hustle, in the success world, is simply believing in yourself, creating a plan, and hustling...until you score points...closer to your goal" (Gray, 2008). This book is a product of my hustle.

"Hold fast to dreams for if dreams die, life is a broken-winged bird that cannot fly" (Forbes, 1995). Likewise perseverance is to pending success as passive income is to reflexive legacy. Generations to come will benefit from what we do today.

"You can methodically analyze past experiences to shape your preparation for current and future undertakings" (Shapiro, 2008). The purpose of sharing many of my life experiences in this book was to shape my story of being smart, broke, and wanting to be a star. Also, it was to document at a timeline a mindset of an aspiring actress before being discovered as a star in reality. In addition, I wondered if anyone else had written a book about their journey to stardom before sensational success and if so, people would not have heard my story. Whoopi Goldberg shared "[i]f something hasn't happened, it's not because it can't happen, or won't; it just hasn't happened yet...I just haven't gotten around to it...I would like to do a lot of things. All I need is time" (Goldberg, 1997). If I could share any seconds with Whoopi Goldberg, I would inform her that I share the same sentiments toward the desire to do so many things. For example, I would like to become a well-known actress, talk-show host, expand my production company, Journey to Stardom Productions in many facets as well as earn a doctorate degree for starters.

In, Is it Just Me? Whoopi Goldberg asked "[w]hy are we so obsessed with pushing our lives out there to be lived in front of a camera...If that's you, what is missing in your life that you need to fill that hole (Goldberg, 2010)? Although she was referring to reality television shows, I pondered those questions as a novice actress, writer, director, and producer. In essence, I conceded that as much attention as I desired throughout my life, I desired more. Then, I read further into her book and she stated, "[s]ometimes they don't get a lot of opportunity to talk about things in depth with folks" (Goldberg, 2010) and that was the epitome of my desire to act, write, direct, and produce.

For example, often, I have wanted to discuss a concept in more detail but the person or group of people had other things on their mind. Case in point, during staff meetings as a teacher, many teachers prioritized what they needed to do in their classrooms as most; and at times the only important task. Professional development for the most part as an educator, I learned that it wasn't received well. I wanted to talk about concepts to help students learn more in-depth and many did not. So many future shows I plan to write, direct, produce and perform in will be about education as well as a form of education to depict nuances that can be developed into learning experiences for students, parents, teachers, and staff members.

Similarly, after researching information that contributed to my mindset and confidence that I can too be an actress, writer, director, and producer, I wanted to share a dream of winning an Emmy nomination like Maya Angelou. "She earned an Emmy nomination for her appearance in Alex Haley's television production of Roots, and she continued her acting career while she developed a writing career as well" (Smith, 2003).

I am thankful to many people for the experiences I have already had and will after this book is completed. I add a special thanks to Spike Lee for being a trailblazer in the film industry; for inspiring me to dream of writing, directing, producing, and being in film. "[T]he most important thing that Spike did," says Lisa Jones, "was that he decided that he did not want to be just an artist, he wanted to create a legacy in a particular industry...he allowed a... generation...access to the industry" (Aftab, 2005). Generations to come of smart, broke, and want to be stars: "Keep your vision present and up to date" (Walsh, 2011).

Notes

Aftab, K. (2005). Spike Lee that's my story and I'm sticking to it. New York: W.W. Norton & Company p.301

Allen, G. R., Hansen, Mark V. (2002).
The one minute millionaire. New York: Harmony Books, p. 360.

Forbes Leadership Library. (1995). Thoughts on success. Chicago: Triumph Books p.56

Gates II, H.L. (2007). Finding Oprah's roots finding your own. New York: Crown Publishers. p.167

Goldberg, W. (1997). Whoopi Goldberg book. New York: Rob Weisbach Books p.232

Goldberg, W. (2010). Is it just me? New York: Hyperion p.46,48

Gray, F. (2008). Conquer the 7 lies blocking you from success get real get rich. New York: Penguin Group p. 241

Henry, M.L., Rogers, L. (2008). How to be a working actor. New York: Back Stage Books p.304

Johnson, E. M. (2008).
32 Ways to be a champion in business. New York: Crown Publishing Group p.13

Levit, A. (2008). How'd you score that gig? New York Ballantine Books p.65

Linkers, J. (2011). Disciplined Dreaming. San Francisco: Jossey-Bass p.205

Littleton, D. (2006). Black comedians on black comedy. New York: Applause Theatre & Cinema Books p.157

Maxwell, J.C. (2002). Running with the giants. Orange: Warner Books p.9

Maxwell, J. C. (2003). Thinking for a change. New York: Warner Business Books p.237, 257

Maxwell, J.C. (2004). Make today count. New York: Hachette Book Group p.13,14

Merriam Webster.com. Teleplay. Retrieved, June 7, 2013.

Nelson, M.Z. (2005). The gospel according to Oprah. Louisville: Westminster John Knox Press p. vii

Perry, T. (2006). Don't make a black woman take off her earrings. New York: Penguin Group p.254

Rause, V., Strickland, B. (2007)
Make the impossible possible. New York: Doubleday p. 217,218

Robbins, A. (1986). Unlimited power. New York: Ballantine Books p. 315

Shapiro, R.M. (2008). Dare to prepare. New York: Crown Publishing Group, p.90

Smith, J.C. (2003). Black firsts. Canton: Visible Ink Press p.743

Spinks, et. al (2008). Prepare to be a millionaire. Deerfield Beach: Health Communications, Inc.

Sullivan, L.E. (2007). Give wings to your dreams. Santa Barbara: Golden Wings Press p.185

Walsh, P. (2011). Love what you have, have what you need, be happier with less. New York: Free Press p.250

Acknowledgements

My parents and family allowed me to make a schedule of telephone calls with them in order to complete this book. Thank you so much for your love, understanding, patience, inspiration, encouragement, and monetary support. Also, thank you for listening during the interim of the many hours of planning and reminiscing. Thank you friends, co-workers, and social media family for allowing me time to write this book. Ultimately, I thank all of the readers for reading about my journey that in essence, I hope will help you and for you to help people. Thank you.

www.ingramcontent.com/pod-product-compliance
Lightning Source LLC
Chambersburg PA
CBHW062001040426
42447CB00010B/1848